Every Valley Exalted

Navigating the Mountains and Valleys with God's Promises

Introduction

As the stirring strains of Handel's "Messiah" fill the air, the tenor's voice ascends, "Every valley shall be exalted..." These words, set to Handel's masterful composition, encapsulate a profound truth found, uniquely, in the season of Advent. Handel, who faced both the valleys of ill health and the mountains of acclaim in his lifetime, knew well the landscape of human experience mirrored in the Scriptures.

This is a journey through the topography of the soul, drawing upon the Biblical narrative that Handel so masterfully echoed in his music.

We start in the valley, a place of humility and repentance, guided by the prophets who spoke of the need for a Savior. As we climb the mountain week by week, we witness the unfolding faithfulness of God, His light piercing through our darkness, His comfort dispelling our despair.

Our path will take us from the silent, expectant streets of Bethlehem to the triumphant salvation song that reverberates through the heavens. We will follow the Sunday Lectionary of the Anglican Church in North America (Year B) as we explore the valleys and mountains of our faith with anticipation of a redeemer so close He might step off the pages of the narrative into our own story.

You're invited to climb these mountains with anticipation, to experience the valleys with patience, and to embrace the full story with a joyous and resolute faith.

For the thinkers and the feelers, the scholars and the seekers, the weary and the hopeful: You are welcomed here, to be challenged and comforted, to explore and to wonder, as we behold the splendor of our King together.

Table of Contents

INTRODUCTION	2
HOW TO SOAP	6
A NOTE TO PARENTS	7
WEEK 1: THE VALLEY OF REPENTANCE AND THE MOUNTAIN OF GOD'S MERCY	8
INTRODUCTION	8
MEMORY VERSE FOR THE WEEK	9
WEEK 1 DAY 1 READ: ISAIAH 64:1-9A	10
WALKING THE STRAIGHT PATH	11
WEEK 1 DAY 2 READ: PSALM 80:1-7	12
THE CRY FOR GOD TO STEP IN	13
WEEK 1 DAY 3 READ: 1 CORINTHIANS 1:1-9	14
GOD'S LIGHT ON A DARK PATH	15
WEEK 1 DAY 4 READ: MARK 13:24-37	16
THE BANNER OF WELCOME	17
WEEK 1 DAY 5 READ: JOEL 2:12-13	18
GOD'S WAIT FOR US	19
WEEK 1 FAMILY DISCUSSION GUIDE	20
"THE POTTER AND THE CLAY"	20
WEEK 2: THE VALLEY OF WAITING AND THE MOUNTAIN OF GOD'S FAITHFULNESS	**24**
INTRODUCTION	24
MEMORY VERSE FOR THE WEEK	25
WEEK 2 DAY 1 READ: ISAIAH 40:1-11	26
THE HALLELUJAH OF THE LOWLY	27
WEEK 2 DAY 2 READ: PSALM 85	28
SHOWERS OF THOUGHT	29
WEEK 2 DAY 3 READ: 2 PETER 3:8-13	30
THE UNFORESEEABLE DAY	31
WEEK 2 DAY 4 READ: MARK 1:1-8	32
A NEW BEGINNING IN THE WILDERNESS	33
WEEK 2 DAY 5 READ: LAMENTATIONS 3:25-26	36
THE WHISPERING SILENCE	37
WEEK 2 FAMILY DISCUSSION GUIDE	38
PREPARING THE WAY	38
WEEK 3: THE VALLEY OF DARKNESS AND THE MOUNTAIN OF GOD'S LIGHT	**42**

Introduction	42
Memory verse for the week	43
Week 3 Day 1 Read: Isaiah 65:17-25	44
Longing for a New Creation	45
Week 3 Day 2 Read: Psalm 126	46
Laughter and Lament: The Fullness of Our Journey	47
Week 3 Day 3 Read: 1 Thessalonians 5:12-24	48
"The Revolutionary Act of Joy"	49
Week 3 Day 4 Read: John 3:22-30	50
"The Path of Humble Decrease"	51
Week 3 Day 5 Read: Psalm 18:28-29	52
"Into the Unknown: The Guiding Hand of God"	53
Week 3 Family Discussion Guide	54
A New Heaven and Earth	54
Week 4: The Valley of Despair and the Mountain of God's Comfort	**58**
Introduction	58
Memory verse for the week	59
Week 4 Day 1 Read: Isaiah 9:1-7	60
"Awaiting the Unseen Dawn"	61
Week 4 Day 2 Read: 2 Samuel 7:1-17	62
Beyond Our Plans: Embracing God's Kingdom	63
Week 4 Day 3 Read: Psalm 132:8-18	64
The Divine Architect: Our Transformation	65
Week 4 Day 4 Read: Romans 16:25-27	66
Awakening to God's Power	67
Week 4 Day 5 Read: 2 Corinthians 1:3-4	68
Finding Strength in the Valley	69
Week 4 Family Discussion Guide	70
"The Light in the Darkness"	70
Week 5: The Valley of Silence and the Mountain of God's Proclamation	**74**
Introduction	74
Memory verse for the week	75
Week 5 Day 1 Read: Isaiah 62:6-12	76
Awaiting True Freedom	77
Week 5 Day 2 Read: Psalm 97	78
The Quest for the Transcendent	79
Week 5 Day 3 Read: Titus 3:4-7	80

BEAUTY IN BROKENNESS	81
WEEK 5 DAY 4 READ: LUKE 2:1-20	82
LIVING THE NATIVITY DAILY	83
WEEK 5 DAY 5 READ: HEBREWS 1:1-4	84
THE HEART OF THE CHRISTMAS STORY	85
WEEK 5 FAMILY DISCUSSION GUIDE	86
"THE WATCHMEN ON THE WALLS"	86
WEEK 6: CHRISTMAS REFLECTION: FROM THE VALLEY OF BETHLEHEM TO THE MOUNTAIN OF SALVATION	**90**
INTRODUCTION	90
MEMORY VERSE FOR THE WEEK	91
WEEK 6 DAY 1 READ: ISAIAH 61:10-62:5	92
CLOTHED IN DIVINE DELIGHT	93
WEEK 6 DAY 2 READ: PSALM 147:12-20	94
SEEKING PEACE IN LIFE'S TURMOIL	95
WEEK 6 DAY 3 READ: GALATIANS 3:23-26; 4:4-7	96
EMBRACED AS GOD'S CHILDREN	97
WEEK 6 DAY 4 READ: JOHN 1:10-18	98
PRESENCE AMONG US: THE INCARNATION'S IMPACT	99
WEEK 6 DAY 5 READ: MATTHEW 2:1-12	100
THE MIGHTY PRESENCE OF THE HUMBLE KING	101
WEEK 6 FAMILY DISCUSSION GUIDE	102
A NEW NAME IN CHRIST	102
ABOUT THE AMERICAN ANGLICAN COUNCIL	**106**
BRINGING CLARITY OUT OF CONFUSION	106
SO WHAT DOES CLARITY LOOK LIKE?	106
WHAT DO WE DO?	106
WHAT'S ESSENTIAL TO US?	106
A WORD FROM OUR PRESIDENT	**107**
OUR STAFF	**108**

How to Soap

SOAP is a method of Bible Study that is easy, practical, and helpful for bringing this ancient text to life in your life.

Scripture

Start by reading the longer section and then focus in on the shorter section. Read the passage slowly and intentionally without skimming or reading too fast. Try reading it two or three times to really get it. Then write in your journal the passage or (at least) a verse, phrase or word stands out or catches your attention.

Observation/Interpretation Questions: (What does it mean?)

Think about the following questions, looking at what the text (in and of itself) means. Don't try to interpret it, yet. Just work to understand what it means on its own terms.

Does the text contain repeated words, phrases and ideas?
Does it mention attributes of God (things that are true about Him)?
Does the text make several points in a row? Number each point as it is introduced in the text.
Did you come across words you don't understand? Mark them with a question mark. Look them up in a dictionary and write a definition or synonym for them in your copy.
Does the passage include key transition words, such as if/then, therefore, likewise, but, because, or in the same way? Draw an arrow to connect a concluding thought to its beginning argument.
Is an idea confusing? Write your question in the margin to address at another time.

Application Questions: (How should it change me?)

Once you've begun to understand the text (or even just understood what your questions might be) then try to apply it to real life. Ask what the passage means for you (individually). The following questions might be helpful. Write what you're thinking in your journal.

What does this passage teach me about God?
How does this aspect of God's character change my view of self?
How does/might this point to Jesus and the Good News that He brings?
What should I do in response?
We can and should draw other application points from the text, but the God-centered questions should always be our starting point.

Prayer: Now, all you need to do is respond in Prayer. Write out something, from the passage, that has made you thankful. Or, write down something that the passage made you sorry about (perhaps it revealed some sin pattern in your life?). Maybe the passage made you think about something that you need from God. Ask him to please provide what you need. This is the TSP model of prayer: Thank you / Sorry / Please

A Note to Parents

We want to encourage you to use the Family Discussion Guides to help frame your Advent celebration as a family. Spending time once a week (or daily with the devotionals) can help build great faith into your family. But, if you're anything like me, family devotions can be daunting!

So, let's start with a few gentle reminders.

First, remember there's no pressure. These discussions are meant to enrich your family time, not to add any stress. Think of everything in the guide as just that—a guide, not a strict set of rules.

Feel free to be flexible and adapt the discussions to suit your family's dynamics and the ages of your children. Every family is unique, and it's perfectly okay to tailor the conversation to fit your needs.

Most importantly, make it your own. The goal is to have meaningful and enjoyable time together, growing in faith and understanding. Your personal touch is what will make these discussions truly special for your family.

And, if you have any challenges, please reach out to us at the American Anglican Council. Everyone on our team has experience with raising children and we understand the ups and downs. Reach out to us at this email: info@americananglican.org for help and we'll do our best to come alongside this important journey with you!

Week 1: The Valley of Repentance and the Mountain of God's Mercy
Introduction

As we embark upon this journey of "Every Valley Exalted," we delve into the profound depths of repentance and ascend to the peaks of God's mercy. We find ourselves in the Valley of Repentance, a place of profound introspection and humility. Isaiah 64:1-9a beckons us to yearn for the divine touch upon the earth, a cry for the heavens to break open.

In Psalm 80:1-7, we encounter the Shepherd of Israel, a plea for restoration and revival. The Apostle Paul, in 1 Corinthians 1:1-9, assures us of God's faithfulness—He will sustain us to the end. In the Gospel of Mark 13:24-37, Jesus calls us to vigilance, to be alert for His return. And the prophet Joel, in Joel 2:12-13, invites us to return to God with all our heart, with fasting, weeping, and mourning.

Together, these passages weave a tapestry of a soul's journey towards divine embrace. Here, in this session titled "The Valley of Repentance and the Mountain of God's Mercy," we are invited to ponder where we stand with the Lord and how we are being shaped and refined by His loving hands. Let us approach this study with open hearts, ready to be molded by the truths we uncover.

In the shadowed valley where we recognize our need for repentance, we see the anticipation of the first Advent of Jesus, the embodiment of God's promise breaking into our reality. He walked this earth and ascended the hill of Calvary, a mountain of mercy unmeasured. As we await His second Advent, our hearts, now stirred by the Holy Spirit through the words of Isaiah, the Psalms, Paul, and the Gospels, long for His returning—where final restoration and justice will flourish.

Each verse from our weekly devotionals points us to Christ, the One who has come and will come again, the Alpha and Omega of our faith, who sustains, redeems, and ultimately transforms our valleys into places of springs.

Memory verse for the week

***Be not so terribly angry,
O Lord, and remember not iniquity forever.***
Isaiah 64:9

Week 1 Day 1 Read: Isaiah 64:1-9a

Isaiah 64:1-9a (ESV) " Oh that you would rend the heavens and come down, that the mountains might quake at your presence— as when fire kindles brushwood and the fire causes water to boil— to make your name known to your adversaries, and that the nations might tremble at your presence! When you did awesome things that we did not look for, you came down, the mountains quaked at your presence. From of old no one has heard or perceived by the ear, no eye has seen a God besides you, who acts for those who wait for him. You meet him who joyfully works righteousness, those who remember you in your ways. Behold, you were angry, and we sinned; in our sins we have been a long time, and shall we be saved? We have all become like one who is unclean, and all our righteous deeds are like a polluted garment. We all fade like a leaf, and our iniquities, like the wind, take us away. There is no one who calls upon your name, who rouses himself to take hold of you; for you have hidden your face from us, and have made us melt in the hand of our iniquities. But now, O Lord, you are our Father; we are the clay, and you are our potter; we are all the work of your hand. Be not so terribly angry, O Lord, and remember not iniquity forever."

S – *Circle, highlight, or underline important words in the Scripture*
O – *Notate observations and questions from the passage.*
A – *Jot down some possible applications from the passage.*
P – *Pray over what you have learned from today's passage.*

Walking the Straight Path
Question:
Why is it so hard to walk the "straight and narrow"?

Reflection:
Humans can't walk in a straight line. There's just something about our inner orientation that causes us to walk in a crooked or warped way. Robert Krulwich, science correspondent for NPR cites a study from Jan Souman, a scientist from Germany, who blindfolded his subjects and asked them to walk for an hour in a straight line. Without exception, people couldn't do it. Of course everybody *thinks* they're walking in a straight line, until they remove the blindfolds and sees their crooked path.

Krulwich observed, *This tendency has been studied now for at least a century. [After animating field tests] you can literally see what happens to men who are blindfolded and told to walk across a field in a straight line, or swim across a lake in a straight line ..., and they couldn't. In the animation, you see them going in these strange loop-de-loops in either direction. Apparently, there's a profound inability in humans to [walk] straight. According to this research, there's only one way we can walk in a straight line: by focusing on something ahead of us—like a building, a landmark, or a mountain. If we can fix our eyes on something ahead of us, we can make ourselves avoid our normal crooked course.* Kurlwich concludes, "Without external cues, there's apparently something in us that makes us turn [from a straight path]."

In our spiritual blindness, we, too, veer off course, our steps curving back to sin's embrace, despite our best intentions. We are like wanderers in the wilderness of our own hearts, seeking direction, yearning for a sign. And here's the Good News -- God has a history of coming down mountains: to save! Christ is the landmark, the mountain in the distance we fix our eyes upon. He descended into the darkest valley to ascend the hill of Calvary and from that high place calls us to follow.

Prayer: Merciful Father, whose compassions fail not and whose faithfulness endures to all generations; Grant us grace to fix our eyes on Jesus, the author and perfecter of our faith. In our wanderings, be our guide; in our transgressions, our pardon; and in our weakness, our strength. Help us to walk the straight path of your commandments, not by our power but by the light of your grace, which leads us home to you. Through Jesus Christ, our Lord, who lives and reigns with you and the Holy Spirit, one God, now and forever. Amen.

Week 1 Day 2 Read: Psalm 80:1-7

Psalm 80:1-7 (ESV) *"Give ear, O Shepherd of Israel, you who lead Joseph like a flock. You who are enthroned upon the cherubim, shine forth. Before Ephraim and Benjamin and Manasseh, stir up your might and come to save us! Restore us, O God; let your face shine, that we may be saved! O Lord God of hosts, how long will you be angry with your people's prayers? You have fed them with the bread of tears and given them tears to drink in full measure. You make us an object of contention for our neighbors, and our enemies laugh among themselves. Restore us, O God of hosts; let your face shine, that we may be saved!"*

S – *Circle, highlight, or underline important words in the Scripture*
O – *Notate observations and questions from the passage.*
A – *Jot down some possible applications from the passage.*
P – *Pray over what you have learned from today's passage.*

The Cry for God to Step In
Question:
Where do you want God to intervene in your life, today?

Reflection:
A number of years ago, according to an article in Preaching Today, a missionary family was helping host a boys' soccer team from Costa Rica. With their advanced ball-handling and passing skills, this elite team reached the finals of the tournament. In that final game they obviously possessed better skills than the other team, a big and physical American team that relied on bullying and cheap shots. Unfortunately, the officials were oblivious to every foul. They called nothing, allowing even outright "muggings." After the Costa Rican boys lost 2-1, I had to restrain myself from yelling at the inept officials. I just wanted them to notice the injustices, intervene like they're supposed to, and make a few calls. Instead, they didn't do their jobs, and the game wasn't played fairly.

Sometimes people feel that way about God and the way God "officiates" the world. We all know that there are big problems: world hunger, a global economic crisis, mistreatment of the poor, political oppression, and worldwide sex trafficking. Then there are also more personal problems: a friend's addiction, a marital crisis, a church split, friends who despise each other. At times we feel like crying out, "Why doesn't God intervene? Why doesn't God make a few calls and keep the game fair? Why does God let the bullies of life win?"
The Psalmist felt that too, calling out for God to shine forth. We're in that crowd, asking for God to show up in our lives, today.

And yet, even when it feels like God's not keeping score, He is. Our cries for fairness aren't just tossed into the wind. He hears, and in His own way, He's moving, even if we can't always see it.

Prayer:
Gracious Lord, Shepherd of our souls, who guides us in paths of righteousness for Your name's sake, we acknowledge our need for Your intervention. In the uneven pitches of our lives, where injustice seems to hold sway, we ask that You would make Your justice known. Shine forth in the dark places, restore what is broken, and lead us back to Your fold. May we trust in Your perfect timing and Your righteous judgment. Through Jesus Christ, our Savior and Redeemer. Amen.

Week 1 Day 3 Read: 1 Corinthians 1:1-9

1 Corinthians 1:1-9 (ESV) " *Paul, called by the will of God to be an apostle of Christ Jesus, and our brother Sosthenes, To the church of God that is in Corinth, to those sanctified in Christ Jesus, called to be saints together with all those who in every place call upon the name of our Lord Jesus Christ, both their Lord and ours: Grace to you and peace from God our Father and the Lord Jesus Christ. I give thanks to my God always for you because of the grace of God that was given you in Christ Jesus, that in every way you were enriched in him in all speech and all knowledge— even as the testimony about Christ was confirmed among you— so that you are not lacking in any gift, as you wait for the revealing of our Lord Jesus Christ, who will sustain you to the end, guiltless in the day of our Lord Jesus Christ. God is faithful, by whom you were called into the fellowship of his Son, Jesus Christ our Lord."*

S – Circle, highlight, or underline important words in the Scripture
O – Notate observations and questions from the passage.
A – Jot down some possible applications from the passage.
P – Pray over what you have learned from today's passage.

God's Light on a Dark Path
Question:
How is God sustaining you, today?

Reflection:

You know those moments when you stumble upon a sunlit spot in the woods and you just have to stop and take it in? C.S. Lewis had a name for that kind of thing: "patches of Godlight." He said, "We—or at least I—shall not be able to adore God on the highest occasions if we have learned no habit of doing so on the lowest. At best, our faith and reason will tell us that He is adorable, but we shall not have found Him so, not have 'tasted and seen.' Any patch of sunlight in a wood will show you something about the sun which you could never get from reading books on astronomy. These pure and spontaneous pleasures are 'patches of Godlight' in the woods of our experience."

So, how's God propping you up today? It's easy to miss those little Godlight moments, especially when everything feels like it's going sideways. Maybe it's that unexpected call from a friend right when you needed it, or finding your keys when you're already late and at your wit's end. Could be He's nudging you through a tough time, like a steady hand on your back. Just keep an eye out for those patches—they're all over the place when you start looking.

Prayer:

Lord of all, who scatters patches of Godlight in the woods of our experience, sustain us this day with your steadfast love. May we find you in every moment, from the smallest to the greatest, and learn the habit of adoration. As we witness your faithfulness, let us be transformed by the grace that strengthens, the hope that anchors, and the love that endures. Keep us steadfast in our faith, awaiting the day of Christ's return, and may we ever taste and see your goodness. In the name of Jesus Christ, we pray. Amen.

Week 1 Day 4 Read: Mark 13:24-37

Mark 13:24-37 (ESV) " "But in those days, after that tribulation, the sun will be darkened, and the moon will not give its light, and the stars will be falling from heaven, and the powers in the heavens will be shaken. And then they will see the Son of Man coming in clouds with great power and glory. And then he will send out the angels and gather his elect from the four winds, from the ends of the earth to the ends of heaven. "From the fig tree learn its lesson: as soon as its branch becomes tender and puts out its leaves, you know that summer is near. So also, when you see these things taking place, you know that he is near, at the very gates. Truly, I say to you, this generation will not pass away until all these things take place. Heaven and earth will pass away, but my words will not pass away. "But concerning that day or that hour, no one knows, not even the angels in heaven, nor the Son, but only the Father. Be on guard, keep awake. For you do not know when the time will come. It is like a man going on a journey, when he leaves home and puts his servants in charge, each with his work, and commands the doorkeeper to stay awake. Therefore stay awake—for you do not know when the master of the house will come, in the evening, or at midnight, or when the rooster crows, or in the morning— lest he come suddenly and find you asleep. And what I say to you I say to all: Stay awake."

S – *Circle, highlight, or underline important words in the Scripture*
O – *Notate observations and questions from the passage.*
A – *Jot down some possible applications from the passage.*
P – *Pray over what you have learned from today's passage.*

The Banner of Welcome
Question:
Are you ready?

Reflection:
Lee Eclov, in a sermon on Heaven, tells a story about Robby Robins, an Air Force pilot, during the first Iraq war. After his 300th mission, he was surprised to be given permission to immediately pull his crew together and fly his plane home. They flew across the ocean to Massachusetts and then had a long drive to western Pennsylvania. They drove all night, and when his buddies dropped him off at his driveway just after sun-up, there was a big banner across the garage—"Welcome Home Dad!" "How did they know?", Eclov asks, "No one had called, and the crew themselves hadn't expected to leave so quickly". Robins relates, "When I walked into the house, the kids, about half dressed for school, screamed, 'Daddy!' Susan came running down the hall—she looked terrific—hair fixed, make-up on, and a crisp yellow dress. 'How did you know?' I asked.
'I didn't,' she answered through tears of joy. 'Once we knew the war was over, we knew you'd be home one of these days. We knew you'd try to surprise us, so we were ready every day.'"
That readiness—that's about a life lived with a constant undercurrent of expectation. It's not about the paralyzing fear of the unknown, but about the daily, ordinary things done with an extraordinary frame of mind. The Robins family teaches us that to be ready is to live with hearts wide open, with love that anticipates, with work that speaks of hope, and with a spirit that looks beyond the horizon.

Prayer:
Loving Father, whose return is certain as the dawn, grant us the grace to live each day with hearts expectant and homes prepared for your coming. May we not be found sleeping but active in love, vigilant in faith, and joyous in hope. Help us to embrace the ordinary with an extraordinary watchfulness, that in the midst of our everyday chores and checklists, we may always be ready to welcome you with joy. In the precious name of Jesus, who will come again in glory, we pray. Amen.

Week 1 Day 5 Read: Joel 2:12-13

Joel 2:12-13 (ESV) *"Yet even now," declares the Lord, "return to me with all your heart, with fasting, with weeping, and with mourning; and rend your hearts and not your garments." Return to the Lord your God, for he is gracious and merciful, slow to anger, and abounding in steadfast love; and he relents over disaster.*

S – *Circle, highlight, or underline important words in the Scripture*
O – *Notate observations and questions from the passage.*
A – *Jot down some possible applications from the passage.*
P – *Pray over what you have learned from today's passage.*

God's wait for us
Question:
Is every part of you ready to return to the Lord? Even the deep dark parts?

Reflection:
In the quiet corners of our hearts, where shadows linger, Joel beckons us with a call as tender as it is urgent: "Return to the Lord your God, for he is gracious and merciful, slow to anger, and abounding in steadfast love..." (Joel 2:12-13). It's an invitation to bring every part of ourselves to God—the good, the bad, and especially the deep dark parts we'd rather forget about.

A. W. Tozer puts it starkly, *"God will take nine steps toward us, but he will not take the tenth. He will incline us to repent, but he cannot do our repenting for us."* God is indeed close, closer than our very breath, yet the final step—turning our hearts back to Him—rests with us.

Certainly, the journey inward can be as daunting as any trek through untamed wilderness. The deep dark parts of our souls, those corners we've not yet surrendered to God's light, beckon us with a promise of true freedom found in vulnerability. It's in this raw honesty, in the silent confession of our hidden selves, that we find the beauty of God's grace made perfect in our weakness. For it's not just the clean, well-lit rooms of our hearts that He wishes to inhabit, but the dusty, forgotten chambers as well. It's a return to the Lord that encompasses our whole being, leaving no stone unturned, no shadow untouched by His healing presence.

Prayer:
Merciful God, who is both tender and fierce in love, draw us to Yourself with cords of kindness. Give us the strength to take the final step in repentance that You call us to make. Let our hearts be rent and not our garments, a true turning in the hidden places where only You see. Cultivate in us a wholeness that longs for Your light in every shadowed part. In the faithfulness of Jesus, we make this prayer. Amen.

Week 1 Family Discussion Guide
"The Potter and the Clay"

Candle Lighting:
Light the first Advent candle.

Opening Prayer:
"Almighty God, as we gather in the warmth of our home and the glow of this candle, prepare our hearts for the coming of Your Son. Guide us out of the valley of our sins and lead us to the mountain of Your mercy. Amen."

Reading:
Isaiah 64:1-9a (ESV) *" Oh that you would rend the heavens and come down, that the mountains might quake at your presence— as when fire kindles brushwood and the fire causes water to boil— to make your name known to your adversaries, and that the nations might tremble at your presence! When you did awesome things that we did not look for, you came down, the mountains quaked at your presence. From of old no one has heard or perceived by the ear, no eye has seen a God besides you, who acts for those who wait for him. You meet him who joyfully works righteousness, those who remember you in your ways. Behold, you were angry, and we sinned; in our sins we have been a long time, and shall we be saved? We have all become like one who is unclean, and all our righteous deeds are like a polluted garment. We all fade like a leaf, and our iniquities, like the wind, take us away. There is no one who calls upon your name, who rouses himself to take hold of you; for you have hidden your face from us, and have made us melt in the hand of our iniquities. But now, O Lord, you are our Father; we are the clay, and you are our potter; we are all the work of your hand. Be not so terribly angry, O Lord, and remember not iniquity forever."*

Questions:
- What does it mean when Isaiah asks God to "rend the heavens and come down"?
- Why do you think Isaiah compares us to clay and God to a potter?
- Can anyone share a time when they felt they were being shaped by God?

Discussion:

Let's explore some deep thoughts from Isaiah's words in the Bible.

. **The Potter's Hands:** Sometimes, when God is shaping us, it might feel a bit uncomfortable. But just like a potter carefully shapes clay, we trust God's wisdom and love in shaping our lives.

. **God's Mighty Presence:** Isaiah asked God to come down to Earth powerfully. We might not see big miracles like mountains moving, but let's look for little signs in our everyday life that show God's power and love.

. **Crafted by God:** We're like clay in God's hands! As we go through this week, let's notice how different things - like what happens to us, our friends, and choices we make - are shaping us. Are we letting God shape us into something wonderful? Remember that being shaped can sometimes feel uncomfortable. Yet, we trust in the Potter's wisdom and love.
Let's keep our hearts open to the ways God is working in our lives, even in the little things.

Activity:

Get some playdough or clay and have each family member try to make something. Discuss how the clay feels in their hands and how it can be molded into various shapes.

Challenge:

This week, be aware of moments when you feel God is shaping you. It could be through a challenge, a lesson, or an unexpected blessing. Write these down, and we'll share what we've discovered next time we gather.

Confession:

Leader: "Let us confess our sins against God and our neighbor." (Allow a moment of silence for reflection.)

Family (together): "Most merciful God, we confess that we have sinned against You in thought, word, and deed, by what we have done, and by what we have left undone. We have not loved You with our whole heart; we have not loved our neighbors as ourselves. We are truly sorry and we humbly repent. For the sake of Your Son Jesus Christ, have mercy on us and forgive us; that we may delight in Your will, and walk in Your ways, to the glory of Your Name. Amen."

Assurance of Pardon:

Leader: "Almighty God has mercy on us, forgive us all your sins through our Lord Jesus Christ, strengthen us in all goodness, and by the power of the Holy Spirit keep us in eternal life. Amen."

Closing Prayer:

"God of mercy, as we journey through this Advent season, help us turn our hearts towards You. Fill our days with anticipation and our nights with reflection, as we await the coming of our Savior. Amen."

Benediction:

Leader: "May the God of hope fill you with all joy and peace in believing, so that by the power of the Holy Spirit you may abound in hope. And the blessing of God Almighty, the Father, the Son, and the Holy Spirit, be among you and remain with you always. Amen."

Week 2: The Valley of Waiting and the Mountain of God's Faithfulness

Introduction

As we step into Week 2 of "Every Valley Exalted," we find ourselves in "The Valley of Waiting and the Mountain of God's Faithfulness." This week, we are invited to contemplate the profound nature of waiting—waiting that is steeped in the assurance of God's unwavering faithfulness.

Our journey begins with Isaiah 40:1-11, where comfort and preparation intertwine, leading us through the wilderness of waiting. In Psalm 85, we find a heartfelt prayer for revival and restoration, and 2 Peter 3:8-13 reminds us of the Lord's patient timing, contrasting our fleeting moments with His eternal perspective. Mark 1:1-8 beckons us to the wilderness again, echoing the cry of John the Baptist preparing the way for the Lord. And in Lamentations 3:25-26, we find solace in waiting quietly for the Lord's salvation.

In each of these passages, we see a tapestry of waiting—waiting not as passive inaction but as an active, hopeful anticipation of God's promises. They point us to Jesus, who in His first Advent came as the long-awaited Messiah, fulfilling the words of the prophets. And as we await His second Advent, we are reminded that in this valley of waiting, we stand on the mountain of God's faithfulness, looking forward to the day when He will make all things new.

In Christ, we find the ultimate fulfillment of God's promises, a sure and steadfast anchor in our times of waiting.

Memory verse for the week

*The grass withers, the flower fades,
but the word of our God will stand forever.*

Isaiah 40:8

Week 2 Day 1 Read: Isaiah 40:1-11

Isaiah 40:1-11 (ESV) *"Comfort, comfort my people, says your God. Speak tenderly to Jerusalem, and cry to her that her warfare is ended, that her iniquity is pardoned, that she has received from the Lord's hand double for all her sins. A voice cries: "In the wilderness prepare the way of the Lord; make straight in the desert a highway for our God. Every valley shall be lifted up, and every mountain and hill be made low; the uneven ground shall become level, and the rough places a plain. And the glory of the Lord shall be revealed, and all flesh shall see it together, for the mouth of the Lord has spoken." A voice says, "Cry!" And I said, "What shall I cry?" All flesh is grass, and all its beauty is like the flower of the field. The grass withers, the flower fades when the breath of the Lord blows on it; surely the people are grass. The grass withers, the flower fades, but the word of our God will stand forever. Go on up to a high mountain, O Zion, herald of good news; lift up your voice with strength, O Jerusalem, herald of good news; lift it up, fear not; say to the cities of Judah, "Behold your God!" Behold, the Lord God comes with might, and his arm rules for him; behold, his reward is with him, and his recompense before him. He will tend his flock like a shepherd; he will gather the lambs in his arms; he will carry them in his bosom, and gently lead those that are with young."*

S – *Circle, highlight, or underline important words in the Scripture*
O – *Notate observations and questions from the passage.*
A – *Jot down some possible applications from the passage.*
P – *Pray over what you have learned from today's passage.*

The Hallelujah of the Lowly

Question:
Where do you need God's comfort in your life?

Reflection:

When Handel wrote the "Hallelujah Chorus," his health and his fortunes had reached the lowest possible ebb. His right side had become paralyzed, and all his money was gone. He was heavily in debt and threatened with imprisonment. He was tempted to give up the fight. The odds seemed entirely too great. And it was then he composed his greatest work--Messiah. Could we not say of Handel that the Spirit entered into him and set him upon his feet?

With the opening words of the Messiah, Handel calls to all who's lives have reached the lowest depths and speaks a word of comfort. He echo's what has been a call from the Lord throughout the ages, a call which says, "no matter how broken your heart, no matter how far away you may be, you can come home, because of God's word; His Power; and His Grace".

Prayer:
Heavenly Father, who comforts us in all our afflictions, let us find solace in Your promise that You are close to the brokenhearted. As Handel lifted his voice in a hallelujah from the depths, help us to offer our own songs of praise amidst our trials. May Your grace fill the valleys of our lives, and may we find peace in Your steadfast love. Guide us by Your word and power, that we might rise again, comforted and strengthened, in Jesus' name, Amen.

Week 2 Day 2 Read: Psalm 85

Psalm 85 (ESV) *"Lord, you were favorable to your land; you restored the fortunes of Jacob. You forgave the iniquity of your people; you covered all their sin. Selah You withdrew all your wrath; you turned from your hot anger. Restore us again, O God of our salvation, and put away your indignation toward us! Will you be angry with us forever? Will you prolong your anger to all generations? Will you not revive us again, that your people may rejoice in you? Show us your steadfast love, O Lord, and grant us your salvation. Let me hear what God the Lord will speak, for he will speak peace to his people, to his saints; but let them not turn back to folly. Surely his salvation is near to those who fear him, that glory may dwell in our land. Steadfast love and faithfulness meet; righteousness and peace kiss each other. Faithfulness springs up from the ground, and righteousness looks down from the sky. Yes, the Lord will give what is good, and our land will yield its increase. Righteousness will go before him and make his footsteps a way."*

S – *Circle, highlight, or underline important words in the Scripture*
O – *Notate observations and questions from the passage.*
A – *Jot down some possible applications from the passage.*
P – *Pray over what you have learned from today's passage.*

Showers of Thought

Question:
How are you quieting yourself, in this Advent season, to hear from the Lord?

Reflection:

Anne Carey and Steve Ward write in USA Today about a 2009 Ketchum Global Research Network Poll. Ketchum asked 1,000 U.S. adults (ages 25-54) what they think about the most while they shower. Here were the top four responses:
1. To-do lists
2. Problems, worries
3. Daydreams
4. Work

What an interesting glimpse into what we obsess over as we wake up in the morning or wind down in the evening—the two times most of us take a shower. While we clean ourselves to start the day, we sully ourselves with stress and disappointment. When we try our best to clear the clutter from our minds with a nice long shower or bath in the evening, we fill our minds to overflowing with thoughts about places to go, people to see, dreams to fulfill. We are a people who can barely go one minute without pondering the many things we feel we need to do, must do, should be doing but are not.

Psalm 85 invites us into a different kind of reflection, a divine pause where we can hear God's voice of peace and promise. As water washes over us, let's allow God's word to cleanse our minds, renew our spirits, and recalibrate our hearts towards His steadfast love and faithfulness.

Prayer:
Lord of all peace, in the quiet moments of our daily routines, speak Your words of life to our hearts. Wash away our anxieties and fears, and in their place, sow the seeds of Your righteousness and peace. May we emerge each day refreshed in spirit and aligned with Your purpose, through the grace of our Lord Jesus Christ, Amen.

Week 2 Day 3 Read: 2 Peter 3:8-13

2 Peter 3:8-13 (ESV) *"But do not overlook this one fact, beloved, that with the Lord one day is as a thousand years, and a thousand years as one day. The Lord is not slow to fulfill his promise as some count slowness, but is patient toward you, not wishing that any should perish, but that all should reach repentance. But the day of the Lord will come like a thief, and then the heavens will pass away with a roar, and the heavenly bodies will be burned up and dissolved, and the earth and the works that are done on it will be exposed. Since all these things are thus to be dissolved, what sort of people ought you to be in lives of holiness and godliness, waiting for and hastening the coming of the day of God, because of which the heavens will be set on fire and dissolved, and the heavenly bodies will melt as they burn! But according to his promise we are waiting for new heavens and a new earth in which righteousness dwells."*

S – *Circle, highlight, or underline important words in the Scripture*
O – *Notate observations and questions from the passage.*
A – *Jot down some possible applications from the passage.*
P – *Pray over what you have learned from today's passage.*

The Unforeseeable Day

Question:
Are you ready for God's judgement?

Reflection:
Frederick Buechner, writing in "Wishful Thinking: A Seeker's ABC" paints a vivid image of the finality of God's judgment, likening it to the closing of a great curtain upon history. He reminds us that Christ, in His unfathomable love, will be the one to usher in this final act.

"The New Testament proclaims that at some unforeseeable time in the future, God will ring down the final curtain on history, and there will come a Day on which all our days and all the judgments upon us and all our judgments upon each other will themselves be judged. The judge will be Christ. In other words, the one who judges us most finally will be the one who loves us most fully."

As we ponder this profound truth, let it stir within us a sense of readiness, a keenness to live in such a way that we look forward to the day of the Lord with anticipation, not trepidation. May this awareness shape our every action and interaction.

Prayer:
Lord God, who commands time itself, teach us to number our days rightly, that we may gain hearts of wisdom. As we contemplate the inevitable arrival of Your divine judgment, let us find comfort in knowing that our Judge is our most loving Savior. Amen.

Week 2 Day 4 Read: Mark 1:1-8

Mark 1:1-8 (ESV) " *The beginning of the gospel of Jesus Christ, the Son of God. As it is written in Isaiah the prophet, "Behold, I send my messenger before your face, who will prepare your way, the voice of one crying in the wilderness: 'Prepare the way of the Lord, make his paths straight,' " John appeared, baptizing in the wilderness and proclaiming a baptism of repentance for the forgiveness of sins. And all the country of Judea and all Jerusalem were going out to him and were being baptized by him in the river Jordan, confessing their sins. Now John was clothed with camel's hair and wore a leather belt around his waist and ate locusts and wild honey. And he preached, saying, "After me comes he who is mightier than I, the strap of whose sandals I am not worthy to stoop down and untie. I have baptized you with water, but he will baptize you with the Holy Spirit."*

S – *Circle, highlight, or underline important words in the Scripture*
O – *Notate observations and questions from the passage.*
A – *Jot down some possible applications from the passage.*
P – *Pray over what you have learned from today's passage.*

A New Beginning in the Wilderness

Question:
What new beginning are you looking to God for?

Reflection:
Auburn Sandstrom, professor of writing from the University of Akron, tells her story in "One Phone Call Changed This Drug Addict's Life"

I was curled up in a fetal position on a filthy carpet in a cluttered apartment. I'm in horrible withdrawal from a drug addiction. I have a little piece of paper. It's dilapidated because I've been folding it and unfolding it. But I could still make out the phone number on it.

I am in a state of bald terror. My husband is out, and trying to get ahold of some of the drugs that we needed. But right behind me, sleeping in the bedroom, is my baby boy. I wasn't going to get a Mother of the Year award. In fact, at the age of 29, I was failing at a lot of things. So, I decided to get clean. I was soon going to lose the most precious thing I'd ever had in my life - that baby boy.

I was so desperate at that moment that I wanted to make use of that phone number – it was something my mother had sent me. She said, "This is a Christian counselor, maybe sometime you could call this person."

It was 2 in the morning, but I punched in the numbers. I heard a man say, "Hello." And I said, "Hi, I got this number from my mother. Uh, do you think you could maybe talk to me?" He said, "Yes, yes, of course. What's going on?"

I told him I was scared, and that my marriage had gotten pretty bad. Before long, I started telling him other truths, like I might have a drug problem. And this man just sat with me and listened and had such a kindness and a gentleness. "Tell me more ... Oh, that must hurt very much." And he stayed up with me the whole night, just being there until the sun rose. By then I was feeling calm. The raw panic had passed. I was feeling OK.

I was very grateful to him, and so I said, "I really appreciate you and what you've done for me tonight. How long have you been a Christian counselor?" There's a long pause. He said, "Auburn, please don't hang up. I'm so afraid to tell you this ... He pauses again. "You got the wrong number. I'm not a therapist, but I've really enjoyed talking with you."

I didn't hang up on him. I never got his name. I never spoke to him again. But the next day I felt like I was shining. I discovered that there was this completely random love in the universe. That it could be unconditional. And that some of it was for me. And it also became possible as a teetotaling, single parent to raise up that precious baby boy into a magnificent young scholar and athlete, who graduated from Princeton in 2013 with honors.

In the deepest, blackest night of despair, if you can get just one pinhole of light ... all of grace rushes in. Just as John the Baptist called out in the wilderness, urging a baptism of repentance, we too are called from our wilderness to embrace a new start. It's in the barrenness that we often hear God's voice most clearly, calling us to transformation and to the baptism of the Holy Spirit.

Prayer:
Gracious God, who called out to us in the wilderness of our lives, guide us to the rivers of new beginnings. May the voice crying out "Prepare the way of the Lord" resonate within us, leading us to repentance and renewal. Baptize us anew with Your Spirit, that we might emerge with hearts ready to receive the fullness of Your grace. In the name of Jesus, who leads us into life everlasting, Amen.

Week 2 Day 5 Read: Lamentations 3:25-26

Lamentations 3:25-26 (ESV) *"The Lord is good to those who wait for him, to the soul who seeks him. It is good that one should wait quietly for the salvation of the Lord."*

S – *Circle, highlight, or underline important words in the Scripture*
O – *Notate observations and questions from the passage.*
A – *Jot down some possible applications from the passage.*
P – *Pray over what you have learned from today's passage.*

The Whispering Silence

Question:
How quietly are you waiting on the Lord?

Reflection:
In the stillness of waiting, the voice of Frederick W. Faber (1814-1863) echoes through time, reminding us of God's gentle whisper: *"There is hardly ever a complete silence in our soul. God is whispering to us well-nigh incessantly. Whenever the sounds of the world die out in the soul, or sink low, then we hear these whisperings of God. He is always whispering to us, only we do not always hear, because of the noise, hurry, and distraction which life causes as it rushes on."*

In the midst of life's clamor, Faber's insight into the quiet whispers of God invites us to consider the profound nature of divine communication. It is not in the grandiose or the tumult where God's voice is most discernible, but in the hushed moments of introspection and the silent interludes of our days. This subtle presence of God in our lives is a gentle but persistent reminder of His steadfast love and the quiet workings of His will.

As we navigate the often noisy journey of life, with its myriad distractions and urgent demands, the discipline of stillness becomes essential. To wait quietly for the Lord's salvation is to cultivate a space within ourselves where His voice is not only heard but also heeded. It is about learning to distinguish the eternal whisper amid the temporal noise, to recognize the sound of truth in a cacophony of uncertainty.

Silence is not the absence of sound but the presence of a deeper listening. It is the ground in which faith takes root and grows, stretching upward toward the light of understanding. Here, in the quiet wait, we are transformed, our impatience gives way to trust, and our restless hearts find rest in God's promises.

Prayer:
Almighty God, in the rush of our lives, grant us the grace to find silence enough to hear Your whispers. May we wait for You with the patience and peace that comes from a steadfast faith, trusting in Your good timing. Help us to seek You in the quiet, in the calm, and in the stillness of each day. In Jesus' name, we wait and pray. Amen.

Week 2 Family Discussion Guide

Preparing the Way

Candle Lighting:
Light the first Advent candle.

Opening Prayer:
"Almighty God, as we gather in the warmth of our home and the glow of this candle, prepare our hearts for the coming of Your Son. Guide us out of the valley of our sins and lead us to the mountain of Your mercy. Amen."

Reading:

Isaiah 40:1-11 (ESV) *"Comfort, comfort my people, says your God. Speak tenderly to Jerusalem, and cry to her that her warfare is ended, that her iniquity is pardoned, that she has received from the Lord's hand double for all her sins. A voice cries: "In the wilderness prepare the way of the Lord; make straight in the desert a highway for our God. Every valley shall be lifted up, and every mountain and hill be made low; the uneven ground shall become level, and the rough places a plain. And the glory of the Lord shall be revealed, and all flesh shall see it together, for the mouth of the Lord has spoken." A voice says, "Cry!" And I said, "What shall I cry?" All flesh is grass, and all its beauty is like the flower of the field. The grass withers, the flower fades when the breath of the Lord blows on it; surely the people are grass. The grass withers, the flower fades, but the word of our God will stand forever. Go on up to a high mountain, O Zion, herald of good news; lift up your voice with strength, O Jerusalem, herald of good news; lift it up, fear not; say to the cities of Judah, "Behold your God!" Behold, the Lord God comes with might, and his arm rules for him; behold, his reward is with him, and his recompense before him. He will tend his flock like a shepherd; he will gather the lambs in his arms; he will carry them in his bosom, and gently lead those that are with young."*

Questions:

- How can we 'prepare the way for the Lord' in our lives and in our home?
- Discuss how God being described as a shepherd gives us a picture of His care.
- What are some "mountains" and "valleys" in our personal lives that need to be made level?

Discussion:

Let's explore something important about how we live our faith.
- **Walking the Talk:** Preparing for the Lord means our actions should match what we believe. This week, let's think of ways we can show our faith through our actions. Maybe we can help someone in need or spend time in prayer.
- **Ups and Downs:** We all face challenges, like big hills to climb or deep valleys to cross. Let's be open about these tough times and see where we need God's help the most.
- **God Our Shepherd:** Like a shepherd takes care of their sheep, God looks after us. Can we remember times when we felt God guiding or protecting us? Sharing these stories can help us see how God is with us, especially when things are hard.

Activity:

Take a family hike or walk in a local park or nature reserve. As you walk, look for uneven paths, hills, and valleys. Discuss how these physical features can symbolize the highs and lows in our lives. While walking, each family member is encouraged to think of ways they can "level" these areas in their own lives to make a straight path for God. Collect small stones or other natural items to bring back as a physical reminder of your commitment.

Challenge:

Identify a personal "mountain" (a challenge) or "valley" (a low point) you want to address this week. Take steps to 'level' this area in your life, whether it's through prayer, action, or seeking help. Write down your experience and be ready to share it with the family at your next devotional gathering.

Confession:

Leader: "Let us confess our sins against God and our neighbor." (Allow a moment of silence for reflection.)

Family (together): "Most merciful God, we confess that we have sinned against You in thought, word, and deed, by what we have done, and by what we have left undone. We have not loved You with our whole heart; we have not loved our neighbors as ourselves. We are truly sorry and we humbly repent. For the sake of Your Son Jesus Christ, have mercy on us and forgive us; that we may delight in Your will, and walk in Your ways, to the glory of Your Name. Amen."

Assurance of Pardon:

Leader: "Almighty God has mercy on us, forgive us all your sins through our Lord Jesus Christ, strengthen us in all goodness, and by the power of the Holy Spirit keep us in eternal life. Amen."

Closing Prayer:

"God of mercy, as we journey through this Advent season, help us turn our hearts towards You. Fill our days with anticipation and our nights with reflection, as we await the coming of our Savior. Amen."

Benediction:

Leader: "May the God of hope fill you with all joy and peace in believing, so that by the power of the Holy Spirit you may abound in hope. And the blessing of God Almighty, the Father, the Son, and the Holy Spirit, be among you and remain with you always. Amen."

Week 3: The Valley of Darkness and the Mountain of God's Light

Introduction

As we journey into Week 3 of our series "Every Valley Exalted," we enter a space rich in contrast: "The Valley of Darkness and the Mountain of God's Light." Here, we explore the transformative power of God's light as it pierces through and overcomes the depths of darkness.

Our exploration begins with Isaiah 65:17-25, where a vision of a new creation promises an end to the sorrow and shadows of the past. In Psalm 126, the joyous restoration from captivity reflects the light of hope in times of despair. The exhortations and encouragements in 1 Thessalonians 5:12-28 remind us of the light we are called to be in a world often shrouded in darkness. John 3:22-30 brings us closer to the source of this light, Jesus Christ, through the testimony of John the Baptist. And finally, Psalm 18:28-29 celebrates God's role in illuminating our darkness.

Each of these scriptures serves as a beacon, guiding us to understand how the light of Christ, who came to us in His first Advent as the Light of the World, continues to shine through us and in our world as we await His triumphant return. In His light, we find the strength to navigate every valley, and in His promises, we find the assurance that no darkness can ever overcome His radiant presence.

Memory verse for the week

> ***For it is you who light my lamp;***
> ***the Lord my God lightens my darkness.***
> Psalm 18:28

Week 3 Day 1 Read: Isaiah 65:17-25

Isaiah 65:17-25 (ESV) *"For behold, I create new heavens and a new earth, and the former things shall not be remembered or come into mind. But be glad and rejoice forever in that which I create; for behold, I create Jerusalem to be a joy, and her people to be a gladness. I will rejoice in Jerusalem and be glad in my people; no more shall be heard in it the sound of weeping and the cry of distress. No more shall there be in it an infant who lives but a few days, or an old man who does not fill out his days, for the young man shall die a hundred years old, and the sinner a hundred years old shall be accursed. They shall build houses and inhabit them; they shall plant vineyards and eat their fruit. They shall not build and another inhabit; they shall not plant and another eat; for like the days of a tree shall the days of my people be, and my chosen shall long enjoy the work of their hands. They shall not labor in vain or bear children for calamity, for they shall be the offspring of the blessed of the Lord, and their descendants with them. Before they call I will answer; while they are yet speaking I will hear. The wolf and the lamb shall graze together; the lion shall eat straw like the ox, and dust shall be the serpent's food. They shall not hurt or destroy in all my holy mountain," says the Lord.*

S – Circle, highlight, or underline important words in the Scripture
O – Notate observations and questions from the passage.
A – Jot down some possible applications from the passage.
P – Pray over what you have learned from today's passage.

Longing for a New Creation

Question:
Do you want Heaven Now?

Reflection:
It's a question that nudges us to ponder the depth of our longing for the divine. In John Ortberg's article, "Our Secret Fears about Heaven", author and professor Lewis Smedes used to ask his students if they wanted to go to heaven when they died. Everyone would raise a hand. Then he'd ask, "Be honest now, who would like to go *today*?"

    A few would raise their hands slowly, giving what they thought was the correct answer, looking around to see if they were the only ones. They were. Most people wanted a rain check. They were ready to die, just not today.

    Then Professor Smedes would ask who would like to see the world set straight once and for all tomorrow: **"No more common colds, no more uncommon cancers. Hungry people would have plenty; no one would lift a finger to harm another; we would be at peace with everyone, even with ourselves. Anybody interested in that?"**

    There would be a frenzy of hand-lifting. Then Smedes would point out that if that new world is what you really want, then heaven's where you'd like to be.

    Isaiah 65:17-25 paints a picture of this heavenly longing, a new creation where the former things are forgotten, where joy and peace flourish. It's a vision of a world set right – no more tears, no more pain, a place where the wolf and the lamb graze together in harmony. Isn't this what our hearts beat for, even when we can't articulate it? The deep-seated yearning for a world free of brokenness, where divine peace touches every corner, is essentially a yearning for heaven, for God's kingdom come.

    In our daily lives, amidst the rush and the routine, we often overlook this innate longing. We busy ourselves with the now, forgetting that our souls are wired for eternity. Yet, in moments of stillness, in the glimpses of beauty and love, our hearts whisper of a deeper desire – for a world made new, a world that echoes the perfection of heaven.

Prayer:
O Lord, Architect of the universe and Healer of our souls, plant within us a deep longing for Your new creation. Help us to see beyond the temporal, to yearn for Your kingdom in its fullness, where Your peace reigns supreme. Guide our hearts towards this heavenly vision, that in our longing, we may find the courage to be agents of Your peace and love in this world. In the name of Jesus Christ, who bridges heaven and earth, we pray. Amen.

Week 3 Day 2 Read: Psalm 126

Psalm 126 (ESV) *"When the Lord restored the fortunes of Zion, we were like those who dream. Then our mouth was filled with laughter, and our tongue with shouts of joy; then they said among the nations, "The Lord has done great things for them." The Lord has done great things for us; we are glad. Restore our fortunes, O Lord, like streams in the Negeb! Those who sow in tears shall reap with shouts of joy! He who goes out weeping, bearing the seed for sowing, shall come home with shouts of joy, bringing his sheaves with him."*

S – *Circle, highlight, or underline important words in the Scripture*
O – *Notate observations and questions from the passage.*
A – *Jot down some possible applications from the passage.*
P – *Pray over what you have learned from today's passage.*

Laughter and Lament: The Fullness of Our Journey

Question:
What made you laugh recently?

Reflection:
Laughter often springs from moments of unexpected joy, a reflection of the heart's lightness. It's a gift, much like the restoration the Psalmist speaks of in Psalm 126, where those who sowed with tears shall reap with shouts of joy. Laughter and joy are not just emotions; they are states of the soul, revealing where our treasures lie.

Brennan Manning poses a compelling question to gauge the heart's true north:

To ascertain where you really are with the Lord, recall what saddened you the past month. Was it the realization that you do not love Jesus enough? That you did not seek his face in prayer often enough? That you did not care for his people enough? Or did you get depressed over a lack of respect, criticism from an authority figure, your finances, a lack of friends, fears about the future, or your bulging waistline?

Conversely, what gladdened you the past month? Reflection on your election to the Christian community? The joy of saying slowly, "Abba, Father"? The afternoon you stole away for two hours with only the gospel as your companion? A small victory over selfishness? Or were the sources of your joy a new car, a Brooks Brothers suit, a great date, great sex, a raise, or a loss of four inches from your waistline?

In the light of Manning's insight, let us reflect on the joy of our salvation, the laughter that springs from a life lived in Christ. As we laugh at the delights of this world, may our deepest joy be rooted in the love of Jesus, who in His first Advent brought heaven to earth and in His anticipated second, will restore all things to perfect joy.

Prayer:
Gracious Father, who turns our mourning into dancing and clothes us with gladness, guide our hearts to find true joy in Your presence. May the laughter that escapes our lips be a testament to the joy of Your work in us. And in our sadness, let us find the solace of Your Spirit, drawing us ever closer to You. In all things, may our joys and sorrows alike point us to Jesus, our source of eternal gladness. Amen.

Week 3 Day 3 Read: 1 Thessalonians 5:12-24

1 Thessalonians 5:12-24 (ESV) *We ask you, brothers, to respect those who labor among you and are over you in the Lord and admonish you, and to esteem them very highly in love because of their work. Be at peace among yourselves. And we urge you, brothers, admonish the idle, encourage the fainthearted, help the weak, be patient with them all. See that no one repays anyone evil for evil, but always seek to do good to one another and to everyone. Rejoice always, pray without ceasing, give thanks in all circumstances; for this is the will of God in Christ Jesus for you. Do not quench the Spirit. Do not despise prophecies, but test everything; hold fast what is good. Abstain from every form of evil. Now may the God of peace himself sanctify you completely, and may your whole spirit and soul and body be kept blameless at the coming of our Lord Jesus Christ. He who calls you is faithful; he will surely do it.*

S – *Circle, highlight, or underline important words in the Scripture*
O – *Notate observations and questions from the passage.*
A – *Jot down some possible applications from the passage.*
P – *Pray over what you have learned from today's passage.*

"The Revolutionary Act of Joy"
Question:
What are you rejoicing about?

Reflection:
In a world where each headline seems to vie for our dismay, finding a foothold for joy can feel like a revolutionary act. In the Apostle Paul's letter to the Thessalonians, he encourages a fledgling church to "rejoice always," a command that might seem as counterintuitive now as it did then.

Laura M. Holson, writing for the New York Times, reflects on this modern paradox:
Joy, it seems, is everywhere these days. It is used to sell boxes at Ikea. It is included in ads for drinks at McDonald's and there are T-shirts that tout joy as "an act of resistance." There is the "Chasing Joy" podcast. And a number of books are being published each year devoted to joyful living, including marriage and productivity.
But if joy is everywhere, why does happiness feel so elusive? Politics in America has divided into two camps: angry and angrier. Our world is threatened by climate change. And the booming United States economy is showing signs of fatigue. Douglas Abrams, author of The Book of Joy, said "In an age of despair, choosing joy is a revolutionary act."

In the midst of this, Paul's words echo louder, urging us to see joy not as a fleeting emotion, but as a state of heart, a persistent undercurrent of gladness rooted in the steadfast love of Christ. It's in His first coming that we find the joy of salvation, and in His promised return, the joy of hope fulfilled.

Prayer:
Lord God, who commands us to rejoice always, plant within us a spirit of enduring joy that transcends the trials and tribulations of our times. May our hearts find gladness in Your unchanging grace and the promise of Your return. Teach us to hold joy as an act of resistance against despair, and in doing so, become beacons of Your light in a weary world. Through Jesus Christ our Lord, Amen.

Week 3 Day 4 Read: John 3:22-30

John 3:22-30 (ESV) *After this Jesus and his disciples went into the Judean countryside, and he remained there with them and was baptizing. John also was baptizing at Aenon near Salim, because water was plentiful there, and people were coming and being baptized (for John had not yet been put in prison). Now a discussion arose between some of John's disciples and a Jew over purification. And they came to John and said to him, "Rabbi, he who was with you across the Jordan, to whom you bore witness—look, he is baptizing, and all are going to him." John answered, "A person cannot receive even one thing unless it is given him from heaven. You yourselves bear me witness, that I said, 'I am not the Christ, but I have been sent before him.' The one who has the bride is the bridegroom. The friend of the bridegroom, who stands and hears him, rejoices greatly at the bridegroom's voice. Therefore this joy of mine is now complete. He must increase, but I must decrease."*

S – Circle, highlight, or underline important words in the Scripture
O – Notate observations and questions from the passage.
A – Jot down some possible applications from the passage.
P – Pray over what you have learned from today's passage.

"The Path of Humble Decrease"
Question:
How can you decrease, today?
Reflection:
John the Baptist delivers a profound statement of humility: "He must increase, but I must decrease." It's a deliberate choice to step aside, to let the light shine on Jesus, the one true Light.

Steven Cole, a pastor reflecting in the magazine Leadership, remembers jogging in the forest near his house when a question popped into his mind: What about John Spurgeon?

I admit, not many people are losing sleep over that question, but I had been reading the autobiography of the famous British preacher, Charles Haddon Spurgeon. I was asking the Lord to bless my ministry like his. And then that question hit me, and I began thinking about John Spurgeon. Ever heard of him?

Until my recent reading, I never had. He was the father of Charles. He was a pastor and the son of a pastor. Yet if his son had not achieved such fame as a preacher, John Spurgeon would have served the Lord faithfully and gone to his grave without notice.

Hundreds of pastors like him have walked with God, shepherded his flock for a lifetime, and gone to their reward without any notice in the sight of the world. As I jogged, I thought, Would I be willing to serve God faithfully and raise up my children to serve him, even if I never achieved any recognition? Even if no one but my own small congregation knew my name?

The more I thought about it, the more I realized, Yes! The Lord never says, "Well done, good and famous servant", but he does say, "Well done, good and faithful servant."

If God makes me as famous as Charles Spurgeon, that's his business. My business is to be as faithful as John Spurgeon.

The heart of this story lies in the seeking of faithfulness over fame, the pursuit of substance over shadows. In our walk with God, may we find contentment in the quiet corners of service, where the applause of heaven drowns out the fleeting praises of earth. As we prepare for Advent, may our focus be on preparing the way for Christ's light to shine, in this season and always.

Prayer:
Father in Heaven, who calls us to lives of quiet faithfulness, help us to decrease that Christ may increase in us. Teach us to find our worth not in recognition, but in the silent acts of love and service that reflect Your Son. May we joyfully embrace the obscurity that often accompanies a life hidden in You, seeking only Your approval, which echoes into eternity. In the humble path of Jesus, we pray. Amen.

Week 3 Day 5 Read: Psalm 18:28-29

Psalm 18:28-29 (ESV) *For it is you who light my lamp; the Lord my God lightens my darkness. For by you I can run against a troop, and by my God I can leap over a wall.*

S – *Circle, highlight, or underline important words in the Scripture*
O – *Notate observations and questions from the passage.*
A – *Jot down some possible applications from the passage.*
P – *Pray over what you have learned from today's passage.*

"Into the Unknown: The Guiding Hand of God"

Question:
Who is lighting your path?

Reflection:
As we journey through life, we often come upon crossroads shrouded in darkness, our next steps hidden from view. At these moments, we long for a light to guide our way, to illuminate the path ahead.

Ravi Zacharias, writing in "If the Foundations be Destroyed" remembered that:

Many years ago, King George VI of England addressed the British commonwealth on New Year's Eve at a moment in history when the whole world stood on the brink of uncertainty. Despondency and uncertainty filled the air. The king's own body was racked by cancer. Before that year was over, his life ended. Unaware of his own physical maladies, he uttered these memorable words:
"I said to the man at the gate of the year, 'Give me a light that I might walk safely into the unknown.' And he said to me, 'Go out into the darkness, and put your hand into the hand of God. It shall be to you safer than the light and better than the known.' "

In Psalm 18, we are assured that it is the Lord who lights our lamp, who brightens our darkness. This promise invites us to trust not in the feeble torches we fashion but in the eternal light of God's presence. As we remember Jesus in this Advent season, we are reminded that He is the light that steps down into our darkness, guiding us safely into the embrace of the Father.

Prayer:
Almighty God, our steadfast Light in the shadows, grant us the courage to put our hand into Yours as we step into the unknown. Remind us that Your guidance is the only light we need, and that in following You, we walk on solid ground. In the name of Jesus Christ, who illuminates our way and leads us home, we pray. Amen.

Week 3 Family Discussion Guide

A New Heaven and Earth

Candle Lighting:
Light the first Advent candle.

Opening Prayer:
"Almighty God, as we gather in the warmth of our home and the glow of this candle, prepare our hearts for the coming of Your Son. Guide us out of the valley of our sins and lead us to the mountain of Your mercy. Amen."

Reading:
Isaiah 65:17-25 (ESV) *"For behold, I create new heavens and a new earth, and the former things shall not be remembered or come into mind. But be glad and rejoice forever in that which I create; for behold, I create Jerusalem to be a joy, and her people to be a gladness. I will rejoice in Jerusalem and be glad in my people; no more shall be heard in it the sound of weeping and the cry of distress. No more shall there be in it an infant who lives but a few days, or an old man who does not fill out his days, for the young man shall die a hundred years old, and the sinner a hundred years old shall be accursed. They shall build houses and inhabit them; they shall plant vineyards and eat their fruit. They shall not build and another inhabit; they shall not plant and another eat; for like the days of a tree shall the days of my people be, and my chosen shall long enjoy the work of their hands. They shall not labor in vain or bear children for calamity, for they shall be the offspring of the blessed of the Lord, and their descendants with them. Before they call I will answer; while they are yet speaking I will hear. The wolf and the lamb shall graze together; the lion shall eat straw like the ox, and dust shall be the serpent's food. They shall not hurt or destroy in all my holy mountain," says the Lord.*

Questions:

- What do you imagine the new heaven and new earth will be like?
- How does this vision of peace and joy impact how we live today?
- What does it mean for there to be no more weeping or distress?
- How can this promise of God's future change our perspective on current struggles?

Discussion:

Let's explore the beautiful future that Isaiah talks about in the Bible.

- **A World Transformed:** Isaiah describes a wonderful world where everything is peaceful and perfect. Imagine a place where animals live in harmony and people are always kind to each other. It's like a dream of the perfect world God wants for us, full of love and joy.
- **Hope in Hard Times:** Sometimes, things can be tough, like when we feel sad or hurt. Isaiah tells us about a time when all the sad things will go away. This promise helps us remember that even when things are hard, there's something amazing waiting for us with God.
- **True Joy:** We often think being happy is about having fun things or doing well at something. But Isaiah tells us about a joy that's even better. It's the happiness we get from knowing God loves us, no matter what. It's a feeling that stays with us always, even when things aren't going so well.

Talking about this helps us remember that God has a beautiful plan for us and that we can find real joy in His love.

Activity:

Using a large sheet of paper, have each family member draw or write their ideas of what the new heaven and new earth might include, such as peaceful landscapes, people helping each other, or animals living in harmony. Once everyone has contributed, hang the mural in a common area as a reminder of God's promises.

Challenge:

Each family member chooses one action this week that reflects the peace and joy of God's future kingdom, like helping a neighbor, caring for nature, or showing kindness in a challenging situation. At the end of the week, come together and share how these actions made you feel and what impact they had on others.

Confession:
Leader: "Let us confess our sins against God and our neighbor." (Allow a moment of silence for reflection.)

Family (together): "Most merciful God, we confess that we have sinned against You in thought, word, and deed, by what we have done, and by what we have left undone. We have not loved You with our whole heart; we have not loved our neighbors as ourselves. We are truly sorry and we humbly repent. For the sake of Your Son Jesus Christ, have mercy on us and forgive us; that we may delight in Your will, and walk in Your ways, to the glory of Your Name. Amen."

Assurance of Pardon:

Leader: "Almighty God has mercy on us, forgive us all your sins through our Lord Jesus Christ, strengthen us in all goodness, and by the power of the Holy Spirit keep us in eternal life. Amen."

Closing Prayer:

"God of mercy, as we journey through this Advent season, help us turn our hearts towards You. Fill our days with anticipation and our nights with reflection, as we await the coming of our Savior. Amen."

Benediction:

Leader: "May the God of hope fill you with all joy and peace in believing, so that by the power of the Holy Spirit you may abound in hope. And the blessing of God Almighty, the Father, the Son, and the Holy Spirit, be among you and remain with you always. Amen."

Week 4: The Valley of Despair and the Mountain of God's Comfort

Introduction

As we embark on this week's study in our series "Every Valley Exalted," we delve into "The Valley of Despair and the Mountain of God's Comfort." This session invites us to traverse the landscape of human despair, a journey marked by trials and longings, and ascend to the heights of divine comfort found in the promises of God.

Our path takes us through Isaiah 9:1-7, where a great light dawns to dispel darkness; 2 Samuel 7:1-17, revealing God's faithful covenant with David; Psalm 132:8-19, echoing the longing for God's dwelling; Romans 16:25-27, which speaks of the revelation of the mystery of Christ; and 2 Corinthians 1:3-4, emphasizing God as the source of all comfort.

In these scriptures, we see a tapestry of hope and fulfillment. The despair in our valleys, be it personal struggles or the collective longings of humanity, is met with the comforting assurance of God's plan, culminating in the advent of Christ. He is the light in our darkness, the fulfillment of God's promises to David, and the comforter of our souls.

For our memory verse this week, let's hold close Isaiah 9:2 - "The people who walked in darkness have seen a great light; those who dwelt in a land of deep darkness, on them has light shone." This verse beautifully captures the essence of our journey from despair to comfort, reminding us of the hope and light that Jesus brings into our world.

Memory verse for the week

*The people who walked in darkness have seen a great light;
those who dwelt in a land of deep darkness,
on them has light shone.*

Isaiah 9:2

Week 4 Day 1 Read: Isaiah 9:1-7

Isaiah 9:1-7 (ESV) *But there will be no gloom for her who was in anguish. In the former time he brought into contempt the land of Zebulun and the land of Naphtali, but in the latter time he has made glorious the way of the sea, the land beyond the Jordan, Galilee of the nations. The people who walked in darkness have seen a great light; those who dwelt in a land of deep darkness, on them has light shone. You have multiplied the nation; you have increased its joy; they rejoice before you as with joy at the harvest, as they are glad when they divide the spoil. For the yoke of his burden, and the staff for his shoulder, the rod of his oppressor, you have broken as on the day of Midian. For every boot of the tramping warrior in battle tumult and every garment rolled in blood will be burned as fuel for the fire. For to us a child is born, to us a son is given; and the government shall be upon his shoulder, and his name shall be called Wonderful Counselor, Mighty God, Everlasting Father, Prince of Peace. Of the increase of his government and of peace there will be no end, on the throne of David and over his kingdom, to establish it and to uphold it with justice and with righteousness from this time forth and forevermore. The zeal of the Lord of hosts will do this.*

S – *Circle, highlight, or underline important words in the Scripture*
O – *Notate observations and questions from the passage.*
A – *Jot down some possible applications from the passage.*
P – *Pray over what you have learned from today's passage.*

"Awaiting the Unseen Dawn"
Question:
What do you hope is on the horizon?

Reflection:
In the stillness of anticipation, our hearts yearn for glimpses of a dawn yet to break. Isaiah 9:1-7 speaks of a great light piercing through profound darkness, a promise of hope and renewal. It is in this waiting, in this expectant pause, that we find the true essence of hope.

Jan Richardson captures this beautifully in her writing in Night Visions: *The season of Advent means there is something on the horizon the likes of which we have never seen before.... What is possible is not to see it, to miss it, to turn just as it brushes past you. And you begin to grasp what it was you missed, like Moses in the cleft of the rock, watching God's [back] fade in the distance. So stay. Sit. Linger. Tarry. Ponder. Wait. Behold. Wonder. There will be time enough for running. For rushing. For worrying. For pushing. For now, stay. Wait. Something is on the horizon.*

As we ponder the birth of Jesus, the light of the world, let us embrace this season of waiting, not as a passive pause, but as a sacred space to behold the unfolding mystery of God's plan.

Prayer:
Lord of Light, in this Advent season, teach us to wait with hope and expectation. Help us to see the signs of Your coming in our lives and in our world. May our hearts be still enough to witness Your glory on the horizon, and may we rejoice in the birth of Jesus, who brings light to our darkness. Amen.

Week 4 Day 2 Read: 2 Samuel 7:1-17

2 Samuel 7:1-17 (ESV) *Now when the king lived in his house and the Lord had given him rest from all his surrounding enemies, the king said to Nathan the prophet, "See now, I dwell in a house of cedar, but the ark of God dwells in a tent." And Nathan said to the king, "Go, do all that is in your heart, for the Lord is with you." But that same night the word of the Lord came to Nathan, "Go and tell my servant David, 'Thus says the Lord: Would you build me a house to dwell in? I have not lived in a house since the day I brought up the people of Israel from Egypt to this day, but I have been moving about in a tent for my dwelling. In all places where I have moved with all the people of Israel, did I speak a word with any of the judges of Israel, whom I commanded to shepherd my people Israel, saying, "Why have you not built me a house of cedar?"' Now, therefore, thus you shall say to my servant David, 'Thus says the Lord of hosts, I took you from the pasture, from following the sheep, that you should be prince over my people Israel. And I have been with you wherever you went and have cut off all your enemies from before you. And I will make for you a great name, like the name of the great ones of the earth. And I will appoint a place for my people Israel and will plant them, so that they may dwell in their own place and be disturbed no more. And violent men shall afflict them no more, as formerly, from the time that I appointed judges over my people Israel. And I will give you rest from all your enemies. Moreover, the Lord declares to you that the Lord will make you a house. When your days are fulfilled and you lie down with your fathers, I will raise up your offspring after you, who shall come from your body, and I will establish his kingdom. He shall build a house for my name, and I will establish the throne of his kingdom forever. I will be to him a father, and he shall be to me a son. When he commits iniquity, I will discipline him with the rod of men, with the stripes of the sons of men, but my steadfast love will not depart from him, as I took it from Saul, whom I put away from before you. And your house and your kingdom shall be made sure forever before me. Your throne shall be established forever.' " In accordance with all these words, and in accordance with all this vision, Nathan spoke to David.*

S – Circle, highlight, or underline important words in the Scripture
O – Notate observations and questions from the passage.
A – Jot down some possible applications from the passage.
P – Pray over what you have learned from today's passage.

Beyond Our Plans: Embracing God's Kingdom

Question:
Do your ambitions fit your hope in God's coming Kingdom?

Reflection:
Living out our hope in God's coming Kingdom requires an understanding that His plans often transcend our expectations and desires. This is exemplified in the story of King David in 2 Samuel 7:1-17, where his intention to build a temple for the Lord is met with an unexpected divine promise.

Dallas Willard poignantly observed, *"'The Lord is my Shepherd' is written on many more tombstones than lives." How often do we echo David's sentiments, yearning to build a house for God, to contain His glory within the walls of our own making, only to realize that God's plans are infinitely grander than our own? David, the shepherd turned king, thought he could honor God by building a physical house, a temple. Yet God, in His divine wisdom, promised to build David a "house" far more enduring—a lineage, a kingdom, an eternal legacy.*

In the same way, our lives are called to reflect not just our personal ambitions for God's kingdom but to align with His grand narrative – a story that culminates in the advent of Jesus Christ, establishing an everlasting kingdom.

Prayer:
Heavenly Father, guide us to align our hopes and actions with Your eternal kingdom. Help us to see beyond our limited plans and to embrace Your grander vision. In Jesus' name, who embodies the promise of Your everlasting kingdom, we pray. Amen.

Week 4 Day 3 Read: Psalm 132:8-18

Psalm 132:8-18 (ESV) *Arise, O Lord, and go to your resting place, you and the ark of your might. Let your priests be clothed with righteousness, and let your saints shout for joy. For the sake of your servant David, do not turn away the face of your anointed one. The Lord swore to David a sure oath from which he will not turn back: "One of the sons of your body I will set on your throne. If your sons keep my covenant and my testimonies that I shall teach them, their sons also forever shall sit on your throne." For the Lord has chosen Zion; he has desired it for his dwelling place: "This is my resting place forever; here I will dwell, for I have desired it. I will abundantly bless her provisions; I will satisfy her poor with bread. Her priests I will clothe with salvation, and her saints will shout for joy. There I will make a horn to sprout for David; I have prepared a lamp for my anointed. His enemies I will clothe with shame, but on him his crown will shine."*

S – *Circle, highlight, or underline important words in the Scripture*
O – *Notate observations and questions from the passage.*
A – *Jot down some possible applications from the passage.*
P – *Pray over what you have learned from today's passage.*

The Divine Architect: Our Transformation

Question:
In what ways are you experiencing God's reconstructive work in you?

Reflection:
As we journey through life, we often wonder about the changes and challenges we face. Psalm 132:8-18 speaks of God's dwelling place, of His presence among us. This Psalm, like our lives, reflects a divine construction, a building of something far greater than we can imagine.

C.S. Lewis, in "Mere Christianity," offers a profound analogy: *Imagine yourself as a living house. God comes in to rebuild that house. At first, perhaps, you can understand what he is doing. He is getting the drains right and stopping the leaks in the roof and so on: you knew that those jobs needed doing and so you are not surprised. But presently he starts knocking the house about in a way that hurts abominably and does not seem to make sense. What on earth is he up to? The explanation is that he is building quite a different house from the one you thought of—throwing out a new wing here, putting on an extra floor there, running up towers, making courtyards. You thought you were going to be made into a decent little cottage, but He is building up a palace. He intends to come and live in it himself.*

In this beautiful depiction, we see that God's work in us is not just repair but a complete transformation. He is turning us into a palace fit for His dwelling. The pain and confusion we sometimes feel are part of a greater plan we may not yet fully understand.

Prayer:
O Lord, our Divine Builder, we submit to Your masterful work in our lives. Though the process may be painful and perplexing, help us to trust in Your design. Shape us into a dwelling place worthy of Your presence. May we embrace the changes You bring, knowing that You are crafting us into a magnificent palace for Your glory. In the name of Jesus Christ, our Cornerstone, we pray. Amen.

Week 4 Day 4 Read: Romans 16:25-27

Romans 16:25-27 (ESV) *Now to him who is able to strengthen you according to my gospel and the preaching of Jesus Christ, according to the revelation of the mystery that was kept secret for long ages but has now been disclosed and through the prophetic writings has been made known to all nations, according to the command of the eternal God, to bring about the obedience of faith— to the only wise God be glory forevermore through Jesus Christ! Amen.*

S – *Circle, highlight, or underline important words in the Scripture*
O – *Notate observations and questions from the passage.*
A – *Jot down some possible applications from the passage.*
P – *Pray over what you have learned from today's passage.*

Awakening to God's Power

Question:
How does the reality of God's power challenge and change your approach to faith?

Reflection:
In our journey of faith, it's crucial to grasp the magnitude of what we believe. Romans 16:25-27 speaks of the mystery hidden for ages but now revealed and made known to all nations. It's about the immense power of God's truth breaking into our reality.

Annie Dillard, in "Teaching a Stone to Talk," provocatively captures a common complacency: *Why do we people in churches seem like cheerful, brainless tourists on a packaged tour of the Absolute? ... On the whole, I do not find Christians, outside of the catacombs, sufficiently sensible of conditions. Does anyone have the foggiest idea what sort of power we so blithely invoke? Or, as I suspect, does no one believe a word of it? The churches are children playing on the floor with their chemistry sets, mixing up a batch of TNT to kill a Sunday morning. It is madness to wear ladies' straw hats and velvet hats to church; we should all be wearing crash helmets. Ushers should issue life preservers and signal flares; they should lash us to our pews. For the sleeping god may wake someday and take offense, or the waking god may draw us out to where we can never return.*

This stark imagery reminds us that the gospel is not a benign, toothless creed, but a transformative, powerful truth that should shake us to our core. It calls us to a deeper awareness and reverence of God's presence in our lives.

Prayer:
Lord God, awaken us to the true power of Your gospel. Help us not to approach You casually but with a deep sense of Your majesty and might. May we live with the awareness that in Christ, we are part of a grand, mysterious plan, beyond our fullest understanding. Amen.

Week 4 Day 5 Read: 2 Corinthians 1:3-4

2 Corinthians 1:3-4 (ESV) *Blessed be the God and Father of our Lord Jesus Christ, the Father of mercies and God of all comfort, who comforts us in all our affliction, so that we may be able to comfort those who are in any affliction, with the comfort with which we ourselves are comforted by God.*

S – *Circle, highlight, or underline important words in the Scripture*
O – *Notate observations and questions from the passage.*
A – *Jot down some possible applications from the passage.*
P – *Pray over what you have learned from today's passage.*

Finding Strength in the Valley

Question:
How does your trust in God change when facing life's valleys?

Reflection:
Trusting God in the valley – the low points of life – is a journey of faith, where we learn to lean on His comfort and strength. 2 Corinthians 1:3-4 speaks to this, describing God as the Father of mercies and God of all comfort.

Amy Carmichael, in "Learning of God," captures the essence of overcoming life's storms: *Everywhere the perpetual endeavour of the enemy of souls is discouragement. If he can get the soul "under the weather," he wins. It is not really what we go through that matters, it is what we go under that breaks us. We can bear anything if only we are kept inwardly victorious. ... If God can make His birds to whistle in drenched and stormy darkness, if He can make His butterflies able to bear up under rain, what can He not do for the heart that trusts Him?*

In these words, we find a powerful reminder: it's not the circumstances that define our faith, but our response to them. Trusting God in the valley means holding onto the belief that He is working in and through every challenge.

Prayer:
O God of all comfort, in our valleys, in our lowest points, help us to trust in Your unwavering care. Like the birds that sing in the rain, grant us the strength to remain inwardly victorious, trusting in Your sovereign plan. Amen.

Week 4 Family Discussion Guide
"The Light in the Darkness"

Candle Lighting:
Light the first Advent candle.

Opening Prayer:
"Almighty God, as we gather in the warmth of our home and the glow of this candle, prepare our hearts for the coming of Your Son. Guide us out of the valley of our sins and lead us to the mountain of Your mercy. Amen."

Reading:
Isaiah 9:1-7 (ESV) *But there will be no gloom for her who was in anguish. In the former time he brought into contempt the land of Zebulun and the land of Naphtali, but in the latter time he has made glorious the way of the sea, the land beyond the Jordan, Galilee of the nations. The people who walked in darkness have seen a great light; those who dwelt in a land of deep darkness, on them has light shone. You have multiplied the nation; you have increased its joy; they rejoice before you as with joy at the harvest, as they are glad when they divide the spoil. For the yoke of his burden, and the staff for his shoulder, the rod of his oppressor, you have broken as on the day of Midian. For every boot of the tramping warrior in battle tumult and every garment rolled in blood will be burned as fuel for the fire. For to us a child is born, to us a son is given; and the government shall be upon his shoulder, and his name shall be called Wonderful Counselor, Mighty God, Everlasting Father, Prince of Peace. Of the increase of his government and of peace there will be no end, on the throne of David and over his kingdom, to establish it and to uphold it with justice and with righteousness from this time forth and forevermore. The zeal of the Lord of hosts will do this.*

Questions:
- What does the image of light in darkness mean to you?
- How is Jesus described in this passage?
- Why do you think light is such a powerful symbol in the Bible?

Discussion:

Let's dive into something really interesting about Jesus and how He's like a guiding light in our lives.

- **Jesus' Many Names:** Did you know Jesus has special titles like "Mighty God" and "Everlasting Father"? Each of these names tells us something special about Him, like how strong He is or how He's always there for us. Let's talk about what these names mean to us and how they show us different sides of Jesus.

- **God's Light in Dark Times:** Have you ever felt better or safer when you remember that Jesus is with you, especially when you're scared or sad? That's like Jesus' light shining in the darkness, making things brighter. Let's share times when we've felt that light.

- **Jesus Guiding Us Today:** Just like a flashlight shows us where to walk in the dark, Jesus' teachings and love help guide us every day. How do you think Jesus' light helps us make good choices or be kind to others?

Talking about these things helps us see how Jesus is with us all the time, guiding us like a bright, shining light.

Activity:

Together, create a simple lantern or candle holder. Decorate it with symbols or words that represent Jesus as the Light of the World. As you work, discuss how this light guides and comforts us.

Challenge:

Throughout the week, be mindful of moments when you feel God's light or guidance in your life. It could be a moment of understanding, peace, or clarity. Share these moments at your next family gathering to see how Jesus' light has been present in each of your lives.

Confession:

Leader: "Let us confess our sins against God and our neighbor." (Allow a moment of silence for reflection.)

Family (together): "Most merciful God, we confess that we have sinned against You in thought, word, and deed, by what we have done, and by what we have left undone. We have not loved You with our whole heart; we have not loved our neighbors as ourselves. We are truly sorry and we humbly repent. For the sake of Your Son Jesus Christ, have mercy on us and forgive us; that we may delight in Your will, and walk in Your ways, to the glory of Your Name. Amen."

Assurance of Pardon:

Leader: "Almighty God has mercy on us, forgive us all your sins through our Lord Jesus Christ, strengthen us in all goodness, and by the power of the Holy Spirit keep us in eternal life. Amen."

Closing Prayer:

"God of mercy, as we journey through this Advent season, help us turn our hearts towards You. Fill our days with anticipation and our nights with reflection, as we await the coming of our Savior. Amen."

Benediction:

Leader: "May the God of hope fill you with all joy and peace in believing, so that by the power of the Holy Spirit you may abound in hope. And the blessing of God Almighty, the Father, the Son, and the Holy Spirit, be among you and remain with you always. Amen."

Week 5: The Valley of Silence and the Mountain of God's Proclamation

Introduction

In this week's exploration of "Every Valley Exalted," we find ourselves in "The Valley of Silence and the Mountain of God's Proclamation," a session that heralds the coming of salvation. Our journey takes us through scriptures that echo with the promise of this profound truth.

Isaiah 62:6-12 speaks of the Lord's proclamation of salvation and redemption. Psalm 97 celebrates the Lord's reign and righteousness. In Titus 3:4-7, we see the kindness and love of God our Savior. Luke 2:1-20 narrates the humble yet glorious birth of Jesus, and Hebrews 1:1-4 emphasizes the supremacy of Christ over the prophets.

These passages, woven together, tell a story of a world waiting in expectant silence, broken by the powerful proclamation of God's salvation through Jesus Christ. His first Advent brought the fulfillment of ancient promises; His second Advent will complete the story of redemption.

For our memory verse, let's carry with us Isaiah 62:11: "Behold, the Lord has proclaimed to the end of the earth: Say to the daughter of Zion, 'Behold, your salvation comes; behold, his reward is with him, and his recompense before him.'" This verse captures the essence of our study - the joyful announcement of salvation, a theme resonating through each day of this week.

Memory verse for the week

Behold, the Lord has proclaimed to the end of the earth: Say to the daughter of Zion, 'Behold, your salvation comes; behold, his reward is with him, and his recompense before him.'
Isaiah 65:11

Week 5 Day 1 Read: Isaiah 62:6-12

Isaiah 62:6-12 (ESV) *On your walls, O Jerusalem, I have set watchmen; all the day and all the night they shall never be silent. You who put the Lord in remembrance, take no rest, and give him no rest until he establishes Jerusalem and makes it a praise in the earth. The Lord has sworn by his right hand and by his mighty arm: "I will not again give your grain to be food for your enemies, and foreigners shall not drink your wine for which you have labored; but those who garner it shall eat it and praise the Lord, and those who gather it shall drink it in the courts of my sanctuary." Go through, go through the gates; prepare the way for the people; build up, build up the highway; clear it of stones; lift up a signal over the peoples. Behold, the Lord has proclaimed to the end of the earth: Say to the daughter of Zion, "Behold, your salvation comes; behold, his reward is with him, and his recompense before him." And they shall be called The Holy People, The Redeemed of the Lord; and you shall be called Sought Out, A City Not Forsaken.*

S – *Circle, highlight, or underline important words in the Scripture*
O – *Notate observations and questions from the passage.*
A – *Jot down some possible applications from the passage.*
P – *Pray over what you have learned from today's passage.*

Awaiting True Freedom

Question:
How does the anticipation of Christ's coming shape your understanding of freedom?

Reflection:
In life's journey, we often find ourselves in a figurative prison, waiting for a door to open. Isaiah 62:6-12 speaks of a profound waiting – for salvation and redemption.

Dietrich Bonhoeffer, reflecting on his imprisonment, wrote: *A prison cell, in which one waits, hopes, does various unessential things, and is completely dependent on the fact that the door of freedom has to be opened from the outside, is not a bad picture of Advent.*

This analogy beautifully captures the essence of Advent. We wait, hope, and depend on God to unlock the door to true freedom – the freedom found in Christ. As Isaiah proclaimed salvation coming to Zion, we too await the fulfillment of this freedom in Christ's return.

Prayer:
Gracious God, as we wait in hopeful expectation, teach us the true meaning of freedom found in You. Open our hearts to the joy and liberation of Your salvation, and guide us to live as people of hope, anticipating the return of Jesus Christ, our Redeemer. Amen.

Week 5 Day 2 Read: Psalm 97

Psalm 97 (ESV) *The Lord reigns, let the earth rejoice; let the many coastlands be glad! Clouds and thick darkness are all around him; righteousness and justice are the foundation of his throne. Fire goes before him and burns up his adversaries all around. His lightnings light up the world; the earth sees and trembles. The mountains melt like wax before the Lord, before the Lord of all the earth. The heavens proclaim his righteousness, and all the peoples see his glory. All worshipers of images are put to shame, who make their boast in worthless idols; worship him, all you gods! Zion hears and is glad, and the daughters of Judah rejoice, because of your judgments, O Lord. For you, O Lord, are most high over all the earth; you are exalted far above all gods. O you who love the Lord, hate evil! He preserves the lives of his saints; he delivers them from the hand of the wicked. Light is sown for the righteous, and joy for the upright in heart. Rejoice in the Lord, O you righteous, and give thanks to his holy name!*

S – *Circle, highlight, or underline important words in the Scripture*
O – *Notate observations and questions from the passage.*
A – *Jot down some possible applications from the passage.*
P – *Pray over what you have learned from today's passage.*

The Quest for the Transcendent

Question:
How does understanding God's transcendence inspire you to rejoice in Him?

Reflection:

Rejoicing in the Lord takes us beyond mere happiness to a profound experience of awe and wonder, as Psalm 97 reveals God's majesty and righteousness.

Gregory of Nyssa in 395 AD described this experience: *Imagine a sheer, steep crag with a projecting edge at the top. Now imagine what a person would probably feel if he put his foot on the edge of this precipice and, looking down into the chasm below, saw no solid footing nor anything to hold on to. This is what I think the soul experiences when it goes beyond its footing in material things, in its quest for that which has no dimension and which exists from all eternity. For here there is nothing it can take hold of, neither place nor time, neither measure nor anything else; our minds cannot approach it. And thus the soul, slipping at every point from what cannot be grasped, becomes dizzy and perplexed and returns once again to what is connatural to it, content now to know merely this about the Transcendent, that it is completely different from the nature of the things that the soul knows.*

In this quest, rejoicing in the Lord means embracing the mystery and majesty of the divine, which goes far beyond our understanding.

Prayer:
O God, who transcends all understanding, guide us to find joy in Your ineffable presence. In the complexities and mysteries of life, let our souls find solace in Your transcendence. Amen.

Week 5 Day 3 Read: Titus 3:4-7

Titus 3:4-7 (ESV) *But when the goodness and loving kindness of God our Savior appeared, he saved us, not because of works done by us in righteousness, but according to his own mercy, by the washing of regeneration and renewal of the Holy Spirit, whom he poured out on us richly through Jesus Christ our Savior, so that being justified by his grace we might become heirs according to the hope of eternal life.*

S – *Circle, highlight, or underline important words in the Scripture*
O – *Notate observations and questions from the passage.*
A – *Jot down some possible applications from the passage.*
P – *Pray over what you have learned from today's passage.*

Beauty in Brokenness

Question:
How does understanding God's redemptive work in our brokenness change your perspective on waiting for God?

Reflection:
In our walk with God, we often grapple with the reality of brokenness. Titus 3:4-7 speaks to us of God's kindness and love, manifesting not despite our brokenness but often through it.

Vance Havner eloquently states: *God uses broken things. Broken soil to produce a crop, broken clouds to give rain, broken grain to give bread, broken bread to give strength. It is the broken alabaster box that gives forth perfume. It is Peter, weeping bitterly, who returns to greater power than ever.*

In these words, we find a profound truth: God's transformative power often works best through our brokenness, turning our weaknesses into strengths and our failures into testimonies.

Prayer:
Heavenly Father, in our brokenness, let Your strength be made perfect. May the pieces of our shattered selves be used by You to create something beautiful, reflecting Your grace and mercy. Amen.

Week 5 Day 4 Read: Luke 2:1-20

Luke 2:1-20 (ESV) *In those days a decree went out from Caesar Augustus that all the world should be registered. This was the first registration when Quirinius was governor of Syria. And all went to be registered, each to his own town. And Joseph also went up from Galilee, from the town of Nazareth, to Judea, to the city of David, which is called Bethlehem, because he was of the house and lineage of David, to be registered with Mary, his betrothed, who was with child. And while they were there, the time came for her to give birth. And she gave birth to her firstborn son and wrapped him in swaddling cloths and laid him in a manger, because there was no place for them in the inn. And in the same region there were shepherds out in the field, keeping watch over their flock by night. And an angel of the Lord appeared to them, and the glory of the Lord shone around them, and they were filled with great fear. And the angel said to them, "Fear not, for behold, I bring you good news of great joy that will be for all the people. For unto you is born this day in the city of David a Savior, who is Christ the Lord. And this will be a sign for you: you will find a baby wrapped in swaddling cloths and lying in a manger." And suddenly there was with the angel a multitude of the heavenly host praising God and saying, "Glory to God in the highest, and on earth peace among those with whom he is pleased!" When the angels went away from them into heaven, the shepherds said to one another, "Let us go over to Bethlehem and see this thing that has happened, which the Lord has made known to us." And they went with haste and found Mary and Joseph, and the baby lying in a manger. And when they saw it, they made known the saying that had been told them concerning this child. And all who heard it wondered at what the shepherds told them. But Mary treasured up all these things, pondering them in her heart. And the shepherds returned, glorifying and praising God for all they had heard and seen, as it had been told them.*

S – Circle, highlight, or underline important words in the Scripture
O – Notate observations and questions from the passage.
A – Jot down some possible applications from the passage.
P – Pray over what you have learned from today's passage.

Living the Nativity Daily

Question:
How does the birth of Jesus manifest in your daily life?

Reflection:
The story of Christ's birth, as narrated in Luke 2:1-20, extends beyond a historical event into our daily lives, challenging us to reflect on how this miraculous occurrence manifests in our everyday actions and decisions.

Corrie ten Boom, a Nazi Holocaust prison survivor, captured this idea powerfully: *If Jesus were born one thousand times in Bethlehem and not in me, then I would still be lost.*

This profound statement invites us to consider how Christ's birth becomes more than just a narrative we recall each Christmas. It's about how His life, teachings, and spirit influence our thoughts, actions, and interactions. Does the compassion, humility, and love of Jesus guide our decisions? Do we find His hope and joy reflected in our words and deeds?

In essence, the birth of Jesus in our hearts should be an ongoing process, continually shaping and reshaping our character. It's in the small acts of kindness, in moments of patience, in gestures of love, and in our pursuit of truth and justice, that we truly celebrate His nativity.

Prayer:
Heavenly Father, as we remember the birth of Your Son, let His presence in our hearts be evident in our daily lives. May the joy, peace, and love that Christ brought into the world be manifested in our actions and interactions. Help us to live each day as a reflection of Your love. Amen.

Week 5 Day 5 Read: Hebrews 1:1-4

Hebrews 1:1-4 (ESV) *Long ago, at many times and in many ways, God spoke to our fathers by the prophets, but in these last days he has spoken to us by his Son, whom he appointed the heir of all things, through whom also he created the world. He is the radiance of the glory of God and the exact imprint of his nature, and he upholds the universe by the word of his power. After making purification for sins, he sat down at the right hand of the Majesty on high, having become as much superior to angels as the name he has inherited is more excellent than theirs.*

S – *Circle, highlight, or underline important words in the Scripture*
O – *Notate observations and questions from the passage.*
A – *Jot down some possible applications from the passage.*
P – *Pray over what you have learned from today's passage.*

The Heart of the Christmas Story

Question:
What's missing in your picture of Christmas?

Reflection:
As we delve into the heart of the Christmas story, let's contemplate our own perceptions and celebrations. Hebrews 1:1-4 introduces us to Jesus as the ultimate expression of God's message, the essence of His nature made human.

Sally Lloyd-Jones reminds us: *There are lots of stories in the Bible, but all the stories are telling one Big Story. The Story of how God loves his children and comes to rescue them. It takes the whole Bible to tell this Story. And at the center of the Story, there is a baby. Every story in the Bible whispers his name. He is like the missing piece in a puzzle—the piece that makes all the other pieces fit together, and suddenly, you can see a beautiful picture.*

Her words encourage us to see beyond the traditional trappings of the season and to recognize that the birth of Jesus is the pivotal moment in a grand, divine narrative. As we prepare our homes and hearts for Christmas, let us ensure that Jesus, the center of this divine story, is not missing from our celebrations. He is the key that unlocks the fullness of God's promise, the thread that weaves through every biblical tale, and the true joy and wonder of Christmas.

Prayer:
Lord, as we celebrate Christmas, help us to focus on the true meaning and the central figure of this holiday – Jesus Christ, Your Son. May our celebrations and reflections be centered around Him, the author and perfecter of our faith. Amen.

Week 5 Family Discussion Guide
"The Watchmen on the Walls"

Candle Lighting:
Light the first Advent candle.

Opening Prayer:
"Almighty God, as we gather in the warmth of our home and the glow of this candle, prepare our hearts for the coming of Your Son. Guide us out of the valley of our sins and lead us to the mountain of Your mercy. Amen."

Reading:
Isaiah 62:6-12 (ESV) *On your walls, O Jerusalem, I have set watchmen; all the day and all the night they shall never be silent. You who put the Lord in remembrance, take no rest, and give him no rest until he establishes Jerusalem and makes it a praise in the earth. The Lord has sworn by his right hand and by his mighty arm: "I will not again give your grain to be food for your enemies, and foreigners shall not drink your wine for which you have labored; but those who garner it shall eat it and praise the Lord, and those who gather it shall drink it in the courts of my sanctuary." Go through, go through the gates; prepare the way for the people; build up, build up the highway; clear it of stones; lift up a signal over the peoples. Behold, the Lord has proclaimed to the end of the earth: Say to the daughter of Zion, "Behold, your salvation comes; behold, his reward is with him, and his recompense before him." And they shall be called The Holy People, The Redeemed of the Lord; and you shall be called Sought Out, A City Not Forsaken.*

Questions:
- What role do watchmen play according to Isaiah?
- How can we be watchful in our faith and everyday life?

Discussion:

Being watchful, just like the watchmen in the Bible, is an important part of showing God's love.

- **Praying for Everyone:** Let's think about how we can pray for others, not just our family. We can pray for our friends, teachers, and even people in faraway places. It's a way of sending love and care, just like a warm hug!

- **Being Alert and Ready:** Just as watchmen are always alert, we too can be vigilant in our faith. This means always being ready to help, show kindness, and do good things, just like heroes in our favorite stories.

- **Noticing God's Work:** Have you ever seen or felt something that made you think, "Wow, God is amazing!"? Let's share those moments. Maybe it was a time you felt extra happy helping someone or when something wonderful happened unexpectedly. In all these ways, we learn to keep our hearts open to God's love and share it with everyone around us. Let's be like watchful heroes, always ready to spread kindness and love!

Activity:

Craft a watchtower together using materials like cardboard or legos. As you build, talk about what each part of the tower might symbolize in your spiritual vigilance.

Challenge:

Choose a specific time each day for watchful prayer. Focus on different topics like family, friends, community, and global issues. At the end of the week, come together and share any insights or feelings experienced during these times of watchful prayer.

Confession:

Leader: "Let us confess our sins against God and our neighbor." (Allow a moment of silence for reflection.)

Family (together): "Most merciful God, we confess that we have sinned against You in thought, word, and deed, by what we have done, and by what we have left undone. We have not loved You with our whole heart; we have not loved our neighbors as ourselves. We are truly sorry and we humbly repent. For the sake of Your Son Jesus Christ, have mercy on us and forgive us; that we may delight in Your will, and walk in Your ways, to the glory of Your Name. Amen."

Assurance of Pardon:

Leader: "Almighty God has mercy on us, forgive us all your sins through our Lord Jesus Christ, strengthen us in all goodness, and by the power of the Holy Spirit keep us in eternal life. Amen."

Closing Prayer:

"God of mercy, as we journey through this Advent season, help us turn our hearts towards You. Fill our days with anticipation and our nights with reflection, as we await the coming of our Savior. Amen."

Benediction:

Leader: "May the God of hope fill you with all joy and peace in believing, so that by the power of the Holy Spirit you may abound in hope. And the blessing of God Almighty, the Father, the Son, and the Holy Spirit, be among you and remain with you always. Amen."

Week 6: Christmas Reflection: From the Valley of Bethlehem to the Mountain of Salvation

Introduction

As we approach the concluding week of our series "Every Valley Exalted," we stand at the cusp of the profound journey "From the Valley of Bethlehem to the Mountain of Salvation." This week, we witness the unfolding of God's magnificent plan as revealed in Jesus.

In Isaiah 61:10-62:3, we are adorned in garments of salvation, a righteousness that shines like a dawn. Isaiah sings this verse anticipating both the salvation God will cover him with and the salvation that will be worn by the Messiah. Psalm 147 extols God's nurturing care for Jerusalem, binding up the brokenhearted. Galatians 3:23-25; 4:4-7 reflects on the law as our guardian until Christ came, so we might receive adoption as sons. John 1:10-18 declares the Word made flesh, dwelling among us full of grace and truth. And Matthew 2:1-12 tells of wise men led to worship the Christ Child, the first fruits of the nations to acknowledge the King.

Each passage guides us from the humble beginnings of Christ's earthly journey in Bethlehem to the universal and eternal implications of His birth, life, death, and resurrection. It's a story that starts in a manger and culminates in an empty tomb, a narrative that spans from a specific point in time and space to the hearts of believers across all ages.

For our memory verse, let us hold close to Isaiah 61:10: "I will greatly rejoice in the Lord; my soul shall exult in my God, for he has clothed me with the garments of salvation; he has covered me with the robe of righteousness." This verse encapsulates the joy and transformation found in God's saving work through Christ, a fitting reflection as we celebrate His first advent and anticipate His return.

Memory verse for the week

I will greatly rejoice in the Lord; my soul shall exult in my God,
for he has clothed me with the garments of salvation;
he has covered me with the robe of righteousness.
Isaiah 61:10

Week 6 Day 1 Read: Isaiah 61:10-62:5

Isaiah 61:10-62:5 (ESV) *I will greatly rejoice in the Lord; my soul shall exult in my God, for he has clothed me with the garments of salvation; he has covered me with the robe of righteousness, as a bridegroom decks himself like a priest with a beautiful headdress, and as a bride adorns herself with her jewels. For as the earth brings forth its sprouts, and as a garden causes what is sown in it to sprout up, so the Lord God will cause righteousness and praise to sprout up before all the nations. For Zion's sake I will not keep silent, and for Jerusalem's sake I will not be quiet, until her righteousness goes forth as brightness, and her salvation as a burning torch. The nations shall see your righteousness, and all the kings your glory, and you shall be called by a new name that the mouth of the Lord will give. You shall be a crown of beauty in the hand of the Lord, and a royal diadem in the hand of your God. You shall no more be termed Forsaken, and your land shall no more be termed Desolate, but you shall be called My Delight Is in Her, and your land Married; for the Lord delights in you, and your land shall be married. For as a young man marries a young woman, so shall your sons marry you, and as the bridegroom rejoices over the bride, so shall your God rejoice over you.*

S – *Circle, highlight, or underline important words in the Scripture*
O – *Notate observations and questions from the passage.*
A – *Jot down some possible applications from the passage.*
P – *Pray over what you have learned from today's passage.*

Clothed in Divine Delight

Question:
What would it mean for God to delight in you?

Reflection:
In Isaiah 61:10-62:5 God clothes his people in garments of salvation, a bridegroom decked with a garland, and a bride adorned with jewels—a vivid illustration of God's delight in His people.

Guido Kuwas, writing for Global Revival News, narrates a gripping testimony: *Hawa Ahmed was a Muslim student in North Africa who became a Christian. She was completely unprepared for what happened. When she told her family she had become a Christian and changed her name to Faith, her father exploded in rage. Her father and brothers stripped her naked and bound her to a chair fixed to a metal plate with which they wanted to electrocute her. Faith asked them to at least lay a Bible in her lap. Her father responded, "If you want to die together with your false religion, so be it." One of her brothers added, "That will show that your religion is powerless." Although they had bound her, she was able to touch a corner of the Bible. She felt a strange peace, as though someone were standing beside her. Her father and brothers pushed the plug into the socket—and nothing happened. They tried four times with various cables, but it was as though the electricity refused to flow. Finally her father, angry and frustrated, hit her and screamed, "You are no longer my daughter."*
Then he threw her into the street, naked. She ran through the streets, humiliated and in pain. People looked at her, curious rather than shocked. Shaking and tearful, she ran to a friend. Her friend let her in, clothed her, and gave her shelter. The next day, her friend asked neighbors what they had thought when they had seen Faith running naked through the streets. "What are you talking about?" they asked. "The girl had a wonderful white dress on. We asked ourselves why someone so beautifully clothed had to run through the streets." God had hidden her nakedness from their eyes, clothing her in a beautiful white dress. Today, Faith is a full-time evangelist with Every Home for Christ.

Faith's story resonates with the transformative power of God's delight. It is not just about acceptance; it is an active, protecting, and passionate force that can change the course of our lives.

Prayer:
Gracious God, may we understand and embrace the joy You find in us. Clothe us with Your love and righteousness, and let Your delight in us be our strength and shield. In Jesus' name. Amen.

Week 6 Day 2 Read: Psalm 147:12-20

Psalm 147:12-20 (ESV) *Praise the Lord, O Jerusalem! Praise your God, O Zion! For he strengthens the bars of your gates; he blesses your children within you. He makes peace in your borders; he fills you with the finest of the wheat. He sends out his command to the earth; his word runs swiftly. He gives snow like wool; he scatters frost like ashes. He hurls down his crystals of ice like crumbs; who can stand before his cold? He sends out his word, and melts them; he makes his wind blow and the waters flow. He declares his word to Jacob, his statutes and rules to Israel. He has not dealt thus with any other nation; they do not know his rules. Praise the Lord!*

S – *Circle, highlight, or underline important words in the Scripture*
O – *Notate observations and questions from the passage.*
A – *Jot down some possible applications from the passage.*
P – *Pray over what you have learned from today's passage.*

Seeking Peace in Life's Turmoil

Question:
In what areas of your life are you seeking God's peace to overcome turmoil?

Reflection:

In the tumult of our daily lives, we often find ourselves searching for peace amidst chaos. Psalm 147:12-20 beautifully illustrates God's power and providence, offering a foundation for such peace.

J.C. Ryle in "Foundations of Faith" writes: *Without justification it is impossible to have real peace. Conscience forbids it. Sin is a mountain between a man and God, and must be taken away. The sense of guilt lies heavy on the heart and must be removed. Unpardoned sin will murder peace. The true Christian knows all this well. His peace arises from a consciousness of his sins being forgiven, and his guilt being put away. ... He has peace with God, because he is justified.*

In these words, Ryle highlights the deep connection between spiritual peace and the justification we find in Christ. This peace, often elusive in our personal, professional, or relational struggles, is attainable as we embrace the forgiveness and redemption offered through Jesus.

Prayer:
Heavenly Father, in the storms of life, be our anchor and our peace. Guide us to find solace and strength in Your justifying grace, knowing that in Christ, we have the ultimate answer to all our turmoil. Amen.

Week 6 Day 3 Read: Galatians 3:23-26; 4:4-7

Galatians 3:23-26; 4:4-7 (ESV) *Now before faith came, we were held captive under the law, imprisoned until the coming faith would be revealed. So then, the law was our guardian until Christ came, in order that we might be justified by faith. But now that faith has come, we are no longer under a guardian, 4:4 But when the fullness of time had come, God sent forth his Son, born of woman, born under the law, to redeem those who were under the law, so that we might receive adoption as sons. And because you are sons, God has sent the Spirit of his Son into our hearts, crying, "Abba! Father!"*

S – Circle, highlight, or underline important words in the Scripture
O – Notate observations and questions from the passage.
A – Jot down some possible applications from the passage.
P – Pray over what you have learned from today's passage.

Embraced as God's Children
Question:
How has understanding your identity as God's child changed your life?
Reflection:
In Galatians 3:23-26; 4:4-7, Paul eloquently describes our transformation through faith in Christ, a journey from being under the law to becoming children of God. This profound change is not just about belief; it's about entering a new, intimate relationship with the Creator.

Bob Russel shares a poignant story: *About twenty years ago there was a house near the entrance of our subdivision that kept their Christmas lights burning long after the season was past. They burned through January. Even through the first of February those outside lights burned every night. Finally, about the middle of February I became a bit critical and said, "If I were too lazy to take my Christmas lights down, I think I'd at least turn them off at night." But about the middle of March there was a sign outside of their house that explained why they'd left the lights on. It said simply, "Welcome home, Jimmy." We learned that family had a son in Vietnam, and they had unashamedly left their Christmas lights on in anticipation of his return.*

This story beautifully illustrates the anticipation and love God has for us. Like the family waiting for Jimmy, God waits for us, His lights of grace perpetually on, welcoming us into His family. Being made a "son" or "daughter" of God means being received into this divine family with unconditional love and grace. It signifies our identity shift from outsiders to beloved members of God's household.

As we reflect on Advent and the coming of Jesus, we see this theme of divine welcome and adoption played out. Christ's coming is the ultimate expression of God's invitation to us, a call to become part of His family and to live in the light of His love.

Prayer:
Heavenly Father, who has revealed Your glory as the Holy Trinity, and united us in the worship of Your majestic oneness, grant us the grace to remain firm in this faith. Protect us from all adversities and guide us in Your truth, as we live each day under Your sovereign care. You reign forever, one God, now and through all ages. Amen.

Week 6 Day 4 Read: John 1:10-18

John 1:10-18 (ESV) *He was in the world, and the world was made through him, yet the world did not know him. He came to his own, and his own people did not receive him. But to all who did receive him, who believed in his name, he gave the right to become children of God, who were born, not of blood nor of the will of the flesh nor of the will of man, but of God. And the Word became flesh and dwelt among us, and we have seen his glory, glory as of the only Son from the Father, full of grace and truth. (John bore witness about him, and cried out, "This was he of whom I said, 'He who comes after me ranks before me, because he was before me.'") For from his fullness we have all received, grace upon grace. For the law was given through Moses; grace and truth came through Jesus Christ. No one has ever seen God; the only God, who is at the Father's side, he has made him known.*

S – *Circle, highlight, or underline important words in the Scripture*
O – *Notate observations and questions from the passage.*
A – *Jot down some possible applications from the passage.*
P – *Pray over what you have learned from today's passage.*

Presence Among Us: The Incarnation's Impact

Question:
What would it mean for Jesus to move into your neighborhood?

Reflection:
Imagine the transformation in our daily lives if we truly grasped the reality of Jesus living among us. John 1:10-18 reveals the awe-inspiring truth of God becoming flesh, dwelling with us, full of grace and truth.

Consider this modern parallel: On Thursday, November 27, 2003—with extraordinary secrecy—President George W. Bush paid a surprise visit to Iraq. His purpose was to thank U.S. troops for "defending the American people from danger." While there, the President served up Thanksgiving dinner to 600 stunned soldiers in a mess hall at Baghdad's airport.

The soldiers had gathered for what they thought would be a speech by chief U.S. administrator, Paul Bremer. Bremer told the troops he would read a Thanksgiving proclamation from the President, then paused and noted that it was customary for the most senior official present to read the President's proclamation. "Is there anybody back there who's more senior?" he asked. The President himself then emerged from behind a curtain as cheering soldiers climbed on chairs and tables to yell their approval.

With regard to this Thanksgiving visit to the soldiers far from home, Bush said, "It's got to be lonely for them. I thought it was important to send that message that we care for them."

In a similar manner, God made a surprise personal visit to the world on that first Christmas—and "the Word became flesh and lived among us." When God wanted to show a sinful world that he cared, he came in person. Even now the impact of the Incarnation should take us by surprise.

Prayer:
O Lord, who in the fullness of time sent your Son to dwell among us, open our eyes to the wonder of His presence. Grant us the grace to live each day in the light of this truth, transforming our ordinary moments into extraordinary encounters with your love. Through Jesus Christ our Lord, who bridged heaven and earth and brought us into your family. Amen.

Week 6 Day 5 Read: Matthew 2:1-12

Matthew 2:1-12 (ESV) *Now after Jesus was born in Bethlehem of Judea in the days of Herod the king, behold, wise men from the east came to Jerusalem, saying, "Where is he who has been born king of the Jews? For we saw his star when it rose and have come to worship him." When Herod the king heard this, he was troubled, and all Jerusalem with him; and assembling all the chief priests and scribes of the people, he inquired of them where the Christ was to be born. They told him, "In Bethlehem of Judea, for so it is written by the prophet: " 'And you, O Bethlehem, in the land of Judah, are by no means least among the rulers of Judah; for from you shall come a ruler who will shepherd my people Israel.' " Then Herod summoned the wise men secretly and ascertained from them what time the star had appeared. And he sent them to Bethlehem, saying, "Go and search diligently for the child, and when you have found him, bring me word, that I too may come and worship him." After listening to the king, they went on their way. And behold, the star that they had seen when it rose went before them until it came to rest over the place where the child was. When they saw the star, they rejoiced exceedingly with great joy. And going into the house, they saw the child with Mary his mother, and they fell down and worshiped him. Then, opening their treasures, they offered him gifts, gold and frankincense and myrrh. And being warned in a dream not to return to Herod, they departed to their own country by another way.*

S – *Circle, highlight, or underline important words in the Scripture*
O – *Notate observations and questions from the passage.*
A – *Jot down some possible applications from the passage.*
P – *Pray over what you have learned from today's passage.*

The Mighty Presence of the Humble King

Question:
How mighty is Jesus in your life?

Reflection:

In Matthew 2:1-12, we witness the magi's journey, led by a star to Jesus, a remarkable event where the heavens themselves announce the birth of a King. This narrative asks us to consider the might of Jesus in our lives, not just as a historical figure, but as an active, powerful presence today.

Warren W. Wiersbe captures this in "His Name is Wonderful":
What a paradox that a babe in a manger should be called mighty! Yet even as a baby, Jesus Christ revealed power. His birth affected the heavens as that star appeared. The star affected the Magi, and they left their homes and made that long journey to Jerusalem. Their announcement shook King Herod and his court. Jesus' birth brought angels from heaven and simple shepherds from their flocks on the hillside. Midnight became midday as the glory of the Lord appeared to men.

This reflection leads us to consider how Jesus' might extends beyond the physical realm. His influence begins at birth and continues through His teachings, His sacrifice, and His ongoing work in our lives.

Prayer:
Almighty God, who in the birth of Jesus revealed Your strength in the guise of weakness, help us to recognize and rely on the power of Christ in our lives. May we see Your hand in the smallest details and the grandest moments, trusting in Jesus, our mighty King. Amen.

Week 6 Family Discussion Guide
A New Name in Christ

Candle Lighting:
Light the first Advent candle.

Opening Prayer:
"Almighty God, as we gather in the warmth of our home and the glow of this candle, prepare our hearts for the coming of Your Son. Guide us out of the valley of our sins and lead us to the mountain of Your mercy. Amen."

Reading:
Isaiah 61:10-62:5 (ESV) *I will greatly rejoice in the Lord; my soul shall exult in my God, for he has clothed me with the garments of salvation; he has covered me with the robe of righteousness, as a bridegroom decks himself like a priest with a beautiful headdress, and as a bride adorns herself with her jewels. For as the earth brings forth its sprouts, and as a garden causes what is sown in it to sprout up, so the Lord God will cause righteousness and praise to sprout up before all the nations. For Zion's sake I will not keep silent, and for Jerusalem's sake I will not be quiet, until her righteousness goes forth as brightness, and her salvation as a burning torch. The nations shall see your righteousness, and all the kings your glory, and you shall be called by a new name that the mouth of the Lord will give. You shall be a crown of beauty in the hand of the Lord, and a royal diadem in the hand of your God. You shall no more be termed Forsaken, and your land shall no more be termed Desolate, but you shall be called My Delight Is in Her, and your land Married; for the Lord delights in you, and your land shall be married. For as a young man marries a young woman, so shall your sons marry you, and as the bridegroom rejoices over the bride, so shall your God rejoice over you.*

Questions:
- What new name does God give His people in this passage?
- How can a name change symbolize a person's transformation?
- What new name would you choose for yourself, reflecting your faith journey?
- Why do you think God places such importance on names?

Discussion:
As we gather together this week, let's delve into the profound significance of names in Scripture. Often, names in the Bible are more than mere labels; they embody a person's character or destiny. Consider how Abraham, originally Abram, became the "father of many nations," and how this change marked a pivotal moment in his journey of faith.

Reflect on the role of names in shaping our identity, both in the physical world and in our spiritual lives. How do our names, or the names we adopt in faith, influence our perception of ourselves and our growth in Christ?

We can explore stories like Jacob becoming Israel after wrestling with God, symbolizing his transformation and new relationship with God. What do these stories tell us about the impact of a God-given identity?

Finally, let's share our own experiences of transformation in faith. If you were to choose a new name to represent your spiritual journey, what would it be and why? How does this new name capture the essence of your growth and relationship with God?

In these discussions, we find a deeper understanding of how God shapes our identities and destinies, much like a potter skillfully molding clay. Let's embrace these moments as opportunities to see ourselves and each other through God's transformative lens.

Activity:

Create artistic name tags with new, faith-inspired names. Decorate these name tags with symbols or designs that represent the meaning behind these names.

Challenge:

Throughout the week, embody the qualities or story behind your new faith-inspired name. At the end of the week, share with each other how living under this name impacted your thoughts, actions, and interactions with others.

Confession:

Leader: "Let us confess our sins against God and our neighbor." (Allow a moment of silence for reflection.)

Family (together): "Most merciful God, we confess that we have sinned against You in thought, word, and deed, by what we have done, and by what we have left undone. We have not loved You with our whole heart; we have not loved our neighbors as ourselves. We are truly sorry and we humbly repent. For the sake of Your Son Jesus Christ, have mercy on us and forgive us; that we may delight in Your will, and walk in Your ways, to the glory of Your Name. Amen."

Assurance of Pardon:

Leader: "Almighty God has mercy on us, forgive us all your sins through our Lord Jesus Christ, strengthen us in all goodness, and by the power of the Holy Spirit keep us in eternal life. Amen."

Closing Prayer:

"God of mercy, as we journey through this Advent season, help us turn our hearts towards You. Fill our days with anticipation and our nights with reflection, as we await the coming of our Savior. Amen."

Benediction:

Leader: "May the God of hope fill you with all joy and peace in believing, so that by the power of the Holy Spirit you may abound in hope. And the blessing of God Almighty, the Father, the Son, and the Holy Spirit, be among you and remain with you always. Amen."

About the American Anglican Council

BRINGING CLARITY OUT OF CONFUSION

SO WHAT DOES CLARITY LOOK LIKE?

We see leaders of local, regional, and national Anglican churches equipped to remaining faithful, courageous, and resilient to their biblical and apostolic roots and together fulfilling Christ's Great Commission in the world.

WHAT DO WE DO?

We build Great Commission Anglican churches in North America and worldwide through
- Developing Faithful Leaders
- Equipping Local Congregations
- and Always Reforming the Church!

WHAT'S ESSENTIAL TO US?

- Biblical Faithfulness
- Prophetic Voice
- Catalytic Leadership
- Apostolic Action
- Contagious Courage
- Holy Integrity
- Prevailing Prayer

A WORD FROM OUR PRESIDENT

The American Anglican Council (AAC) is a network of individuals, parishes, and ministries who affirm biblical authority and Christian orthodoxy within the Anglican Communion. For 20 years the AAC has promoted and defended Biblical Anglicanism in North America and around the world.

The Anglican Communion is among the world's largest Christian denominations with over 55 million active participants. Sadly, this great church is threatened by false, un-Christian teachings, with the authority of Holy Scripture, the Gospel of Jesus Christ, and the doctrine of marriage all under attack. In North America, many Anglican churches are in need of revitalization. While some parishes are thriving, others are losing members.

We want these churches to be fully functioning outposts of God's Kingdom and are committed to partnering with local, diocesan, and provincial churches to meet these challenges by developing faithful leaders, equipping local congregations, and always reforming the Church!

At AmericanAnglican.org you'll be able to see what we do in each of these areas and keep up to date on what's happening in this great reformation of the Anglican Communion. Are you in a congregation in need of fresh vision and revitalization? Are you a priest who could benefit from a coaching relationship with a fellow priest? Do you want to know more about Anglicanism or want to find a Christ-centered congregation where you can serve and worship?

These are questions we often answer. Feel free to email us if you have any questions and please pray for our ministry here and for what God is doing in the Anglican Communion.

In Christ's Service,

The Rev. Canon Phil Ashey
President & CEO, American Anglican Council

OUR STAFF

THE REV. CANON J. PHILIP ASHEY
PRESIDENT & CHIEF EXECUTIVE OFFICER
Canon Phil Ashey is the President and Chief Executive Officer of the American Anglican Council. Phil grew up in a Christian family, a "priest's kid" and gave his life to Christ in 1968. A graduate of Stanford and Loyola Law School, he served as a Deputy DA in Orange County California. He was ordained to the priesthood in 1988, and spent twenty years leading Episcopal and Anglican congregations of all sizes in California, Virginia and Pittsburgh—thirteen as a Rector and Church planter, and seven as a Senior Associate. Phil's focus and passion is to develop Biblically faithful leaders at all levels of the Church—both here in North America and across the Anglican Communion. In 2015 he received his LLM in Canon Law from Cardiff University (Wales UK) and now serves as Special Counsel to the Archbishop, Advisor to the GAFCON Primates, and leads Lawyers Networks in both ACNA and Gafcon. He is also the author of Anglican Conciliarism: The Church Meeting to Decide Together (2017, Anglican House).

THE REV. CANON MARK ELDREDGE
DIRECTOR OF ANGLICAN REVITALIZATION MINISTRIES
Mark was born near Buffalo, NY but grew up in Palm Coast, FL. He received his Bachelor of Science from Florida State University and his Master of Divinity from Trinity School for Ministry in Ambridge, PA. After serving as an Associate Priest for three years at an Episcopal Church in Midland, TX, Mark moved to Jacksonville to be the Senior Pastor of Epiphany Episcopal Church. While leading that church through revitalization, he also moved the church into what has become the Anglican Church of North America. After 14 years in that church, Mark is now the

Director of Church Revitalization for the American Anglican Council serving the Anglican Church in North America by helping local congregations better fulfill the Great Commission in our times. He also serves a similar role as the Canon for Congregational Health for the Gulf Atlantic Diocese based in Jacksonville, FL. Mark is married to his best friend, Ame, has three children from 26 to 16, and one grandson.

THE REV. BEV MUEFFELMANN
DIRECTOR OF THE DANIEL LEADERSHIP INSTITUTE
Bev is a native of the Washington, DC suburbs and graduated from the University of Maryland, College Park with a degree in Psychology. She and her husband, Greg, helped form and were the first strategy coordinators of Anglican Frontier Missions. In her role with the AAC, she directs the Daniel Leadership Institute which encompasses the Lay Leadership Academy, the Clergy Leadership Academy, and the Bishops Leadership Academy. Additionally, she supports Canon Ashey in responsibilities related to the international Bishops Leadership Summit and the Anglican Legal Society. She and Greg are active in the ministries of Holy Trinity Anglican Church, Raleigh, NC and have three adult children and three grandchildren.

FRANCIS CAPITANIO
DIRECTOR OF COMMUNICATIONS
Francis worked as Communications Director and Assistant to the Bishop of the Anglican Diocese in New England (ADNE) for almost six years. He wrote and worked extensively for the Communications teams of both the Anglican Church in North America (ACNA) and GAFCON, participating in and helping to communicate newsworthy events around the Anglican Communion. Before working

in the ADNE, Francis worked as a fisheries biologist for the National Oceanic and Atmospheric Administration, where he got a lot of time to read and write books while floating out at sea on fishing boats. His first novel, Mariner's Hollow, was published in 2014 and won the Benjamin Franklin Award for Young Adult Fiction.

NINA BROWN-PERRY
ADMINISTRATION MANAGER

Mrs. Nina Perry is Administration Manager for the American Anglican Council and has been with the AAC since 2005. Nina provides support for staff and donors/constituents as well as processes contributions and coordinates various events. Nina is a college graduate, is active in her local church, is a married mother of four and enjoys spending time with her grandchildren.

THE REV. GREG SMITH
DEVELOPMENT MANAGER

Greg is passionate about welcoming people home with Good News about a Great God. With over 25 years experience, he also serves at St. Michael's Church in Charleston as an assistant rector for evangelism and discipleship. He has previously served as a rector of two churches, church planter, and as the Anglican Chaplain at The Citadel's St. Alban's Chapel. Additionally, served as an executive vice president with Apartment Life. Greg graduated from Wheaton College in Chicago with a Bachelor of Music and holds an MDiv from Trinity School for Ministry. Greg has also worked as a paramedic/firefighter on Chicago's near north side where he learned the value of teamwork and rapid assessment of problems and solutions. Greg and his wife Anna have been married for almost 30 years and love trying to keep up with their three amazing children.

Made in the USA
Columbia, SC
19 November 2023